T0149682

MANUFACTURING 4.0

MANUFACTURING 4.0

THE USE OF EMERGENT TECHNOLOGIES IN MANUFACTURING

O. Perez / S. Sauceda / J. Cruz

Library of Congress Control Number: 2018908878
ISBN: Hardcover   978-1-5065-2617-1
                   Softcover   978-1-5065-2618-8
                   eBook   978-1-5065-2619-5

Print information available on the last page.

Rev. date: 06/08/2018

To order additional copies of this book, contact:
Palibrio
1663 Liberty Drive
Suite 200
Bloomington, IN 47403
Toll Free from the U.S.A 877.407.5847
Toll Free from Mexico 01.800.288.2243
Toll Free from Spain 900.866.949
From other International locations +1.812.671.9757
Fax: 01.812.355.1576
orders@palibrio.com
782112

CONTENTS

Thank You Note

Thanks to my friends Sergio and Jesrael for the hours dedicated to this book and my family: Ely, Abraham, Claire and Megan.

O.Perez

Thanks to Oliver (my mentor) and Jesrael for sharing same technical philosophy & collaborate to make this book a reality. You guys share a passion and spirit for innovation, you really rock.

Special thanks to my grandmother Nico (RIP), my mother Nelly (the strongest pillar in my life), my sister Jaret, my uncles Cruz and Diego, my aunt Elea (RIP) for all the love, support and for teaching me how the world rules.

- To my "raza" Bernarda and "Don Jesus" (RIP) whom have been important piece of my life.

- To my two biggest reasons that make the difference in my life! Romina and Roman.

- To my father Sergio for all his love & support.

- To that special day, when Alejandrina changed me the way to see the world.

- To Marina, for all her support & love. You are awesome, unique and special. Please never forget that!

- To all my friends, family & colleagues that have been part of my human & professional growth.

Totally grateful with God, my lord, for letting me live this fantastic, perfectly imperfect life!

S Sauceda

Thanks to Dr. Perez and M.Sc. Sauceda for the opportunity to collaborate with them on the making of this book and to all the people that shared with me all their invaluable knowledge throughout these years and that have shaped the way I now see the manufacturing world.

And finally thanks to my wife Belem for her patience and support and to my children Citlaly and Edrei, may this book help them better understand the potential of the IoT beyond their gaming console!

J. Cruz.

Foreword from Mario Rivera

I AM DELIGHTED to write this foreword, not only because Dr. Oliver Perez has been a friend and colleague for nearly twenty years, but because I'm a strong advocate for the educational value that this text will bring to students, individual contributors, and leaders that will inevitably be part of the 4th industrial revolution that is taking place in the twenty-first century.

The book will guide the reader through the history of the industrial era, the evolution of our industrial systems, and perhaps more importantly, through a pragmatic approach on how to integrate the proven value of Lean with more recent technologies that will help modernize operations across all industry segments.

Dr. Perez, Sauceda and Cruz are a proven technology leaders in the Medical Technology industry who has collected a number of hands-on experiences assessing, road-mapping, and deploying Lean based solutions to simplify manufacturing operations of complex products, from active implantable medical device components & sub-assemblies, to electro-mechanical instruments & capital equipment, to large volume consumable products used in diverse medical applications.

More recently, Dr. Perez, Sauceda and Cruz have embarked in an exciting technological journey that has allowed them to develop strong business cases to invest in manufacturing technologies such as manufacturing execution systems, augmented reality, and real-time data & analytics to improve operational performance and drive increased profitability.

After reading this book, you will find it hard to defend the status quo and will come to realize that our economy and our industry is inevitably moving towards higher digitalization and frequent technology advancements that will require you to be willing and able to adapt to change at a faster pace, and deal with higher levels of volatility, uncertainty, complexity, and ambiguity.

The entire text will serve as a valuable reference on the main technologies that encompass the realm of Industry 4.0, and more specifically those that are applicable in a manufacturing environment, or Manufacturing 4.0.

I hope that this book will become a primer for students pursuing technical degrees, engineers, scientists, supply chain professionals, industry leaders, and manufacturing enthusiasts around the world to learn what Manufacturing 4.0 entails and how to merge it into their day to day operations.

Mario Rivera-Becerra

Vice President, Operations & Supply Chain

Foreword from Carlos López Monsalvo

This book is clear, concrete and practical for manufacturing leaders and specialists. It is an open invitation to MMCA (Make Manufacturing Cool Again). This is a real-world proposal and welcome for commodity companies to change their mindset.

To understand, by implementing emerging technologies in manufacturing not only influence operations indicators like quality, cost, safety, and delivery but also the time for the company to innovate and transform it into a Smart company.

This book is more than a guidance to be more productive with technology. The authors draft a strategic framework to move to a new stage in the innovation journey and the management of technology to be competitive in a complex voracious world.

The book provides practical tools and examples that drive like building blocks a new scenario to enterprises.

Carlos López Monsalvo

National Technology Award Foundation, Former President of the Technical Board

Foreword from the authors

GRATITUDE IS THE genesis of this book that goes back to the skills and knowledge acquired, stresses, frustrations and satisfactions experienced during the implementations of multiple process technology projects through our careers. We have enormous appreciation to the engineers, technicians and supporters that motivated us and let us know that to know something is good but to do something with what you know is what really matters, it is then that the impact is relevant.

The most important task of a leader is to pass on that knowledge, to train and form a new wave of leaders that will reach further frontiers. The main reason we started this book is to document this knowledge and talk directly to the brain and heart of that pipeline of leaders working to bring their factories into the 21st century. Francis Bacon is attributed with the phrase "Knowledge is Power" back in 1579. Today, power is no longer just in the knowledge but in the tangible value you add to your organization with that knowledge. It is egotistical to know and do not act, it is better to be a contributor on this constantly changing environment than wait for the change to explode in our face.

The goal of this book to provide guidance, examples, and analyze the trends and capabilities of the impact of Industry 4.0 solely in manufacturing. Unveil the steps that the spearheading companies took and pass them in this book in order to prevent you to fall into the group of laggards playing catch up. At the same time this book expectation is to serve as a guide for Engineers, project leaders and executives on the implementation of Manufacturing 4.0 technologies in their facilities to support their Continuous Improvement Journey.

It is broadly documented the four transformations leading to Industry 4.0, it is not the goal of this book to describe four stages of manufacturing to justify manufacturing 4.0. For us, the term is simply explained as the creation of value in manufacturing by the use of the tools, methods, and technologies brought to the world by the industry 4.0 wave.

Another objective of this document is to exhibit the reasons why manufacturing 4.0 must be an important priority for all companies, and why it should be in top of the mind of leaders to provide a clear vision to the rest of the organization.

In the first section, we approach the topic of manufacturing as a concept that carries a long history of successes and pitfalls. It is with great respect that we dare to address briefly in the first chapter its meaning and its transformation across the time always looking for higher levels of productivity. We describe how along the time different actors improved the way we convert a set of raw materials into a profitable appealing product until our days. The readers will discover that manufacturing evolved but also became complex because of different forces ruling today's markets, technologies availabilities and customers desires. The convergence of these forces created a huge impact in manufacturing and the struggle to counter power these forces by the current industrial methodologies is evident so new capacities needed to be added to our production systems to once again propel productivity to the next stage. Those new capacities are a set of process technology enablers result of the rise of industry 4.0. At the end of this section, we explain how these methodologies such Lean manufacturing focusing in waste reduction aren't in contradiction with these enablers but complement them, and we encourage the reader to use them in tandem depending of the situation of its production system.

On the second segment, we deliver a simple way to assess your current production. We have found that it is necessary to know where to start, to recognize that manufacturing 4.0 journey is just the beginning and that it is necessary to understand what problem to tackle first and why, to build the manufacturing 4.0 roadmap of your factory. We define a simple nomenclature of a manufacturing site with the different functions and directly apply questions to evaluate those functions. At the end of the assessment, the auditor will know what areas are leading the transformation, which ones are lagging behind and on what technologies. The goal is to provide a tool that clearly states the situation and provides light where to start.

Segment three, reaffirms manufacturing 4.0 as a subset of Industry 4.0 and groups the concepts in three pillars: Digitalization, Robotization, and Additive Manufacturing. This section describes digital technologies in detail for each of the technologies grouped under this pillar, and explains the reason why digitalization is an imperative, shows examples of applications in manufacturing as well as a brief explanation of the standards if available.

Subsections for technologies such as the Internet of Things, Artificial Intelligence, Augmented Reality, Manufacturing Execution Systems, Automated Data Collection and others are depicted here.

The fourth segment starts with a section on robotics strategy and why it is imperative for all the companies to make such strategy available for their companies. Why it isn't optional to continue delaying robotics implementation and how the transformation of the production floor is happening at a fast speed. What are the forces driving such change, and why understand them will make your technology projects essential. Subsections for Collaborative Robots, Autonomous Mobile Robots exoskeletons are part of it.

Fifth section is called additive Manufacturing. Here we outline a strategy and the potential opportunities you can tackle with this emergent technology. It shows the progress of three dimensional printing and its impact in manufacturing. We start by describing the transformation from subtractive to additive and by understanding the state of the art of this technology and some ideas to apply it in manufacturing to vertically integrate your material supply.

Finally, a section called **Humanity 4.X** describing the impact of manufacturing 4.0 in other areas such the environment, leadership, and education are reviewed, recognizing that the interactions between the human elements, and technology within a manufacturing surrounding are important, and most importantly that the impact of technology on these areas can't be neglected. A clear message for the C-Suite to be prepared or *laissez faire*.

We close the book with the expectation that you, the reader have now another set of tools ready to go out to your production floor to make it more productive able to differentiate excitement from reality and with a clear picture (after the assessment) of the pain points your facility experience. You have the tools, and know where to start, the ball is in your court.

Our ultimate goal is that by skimming through the different sections of this book the reader will have the sensation that doing a technology project applied to manufacturing processes using manufacturing 4.0 enablers is within reach, that adding value is possible and it is simpler than it looks.

Introduction

WITH TECHNOLOGIES ADVANCING at breakneck speeds, robotics, artificial intelligence, augmented reality, data analytics, and others are finding new applications in factories. As operations leader your quest to find better quality levels, cost efficiencies and the constant concern about your employee's safety and health never ends.

So the question is: How can we harness all these technologies to improve the operation? How can we extract what is on the fringes still to be proven to provide sustainable, best in class across all the operation, from interfacing with the supplier up to the distribution of the finish goods.

By implementing emergent technologies, we aren't only providing value to the operation for Safety, Quality, Delivery and Cost, we are also preparing the operation for an inevitable use of concepts, technologies and principles that will govern factories in the near future. So let's talk about the manufacturing transformation is taking place around the world and the emergent technologies that are blossoming. Let's talk about technology as a driver for Operational Excellence and the role of humans in this scenario, what are the new set of skills required for the engineers to succeed in this technology wave.

Let's talk about the Smart use of manufacturing data to increase visibility in order to manage production assets, or to harvest it for Continuous Improvement purposes or attach it to components for traceability or collect it from the floor for compliance purposes.

Let's talk about inventory data that allow us to communicate better with suppliers to prevent shortages and maintain healthy raw material reducing exposition. The data that for years has been inefficiently transcribed from Kanban cards to spreadsheets, from forms into databases, and that sometimes put us in trouble during audits, yes, let's talk about the tons of data coming out of the production floor, the data coming out of the quality activities, the data issued every day and how to tame this enormous amount a data but above all, let's talk about how to give a purpose to the collection and use of it.

Or the use of Robots that can collaborate arm to arm with our associate in the production floor instead of have them in cages isolated with restricted contributions, now we can explore collaborative environments in order to reduce cycle time and rebalance the lines and increase throughput.

Or Autonomous Mobile Robots that can deliver to our exact location the right part, at the right time directly from the warehouse without human intervention. Or this same technology that can help us to move heavy products or components from point A to point B effortlessly.

Or about exoskeletons that can prevent injuries when transferring heavy components during the manufacturing of heavy products.

If three dimensional printing can demonstrate its applicability for manufacturing it is on the low volume environments where it has the most promising potential. Reducing procurement overhead, integrating vertically and reducing risk of last time buys or complex pricy parts.

What if we use Artificial Intelligence (AI) to improve inspection? By integrating AI into inspection using Neural networks for machine learning, we are giving the inspection a competitive advantage that can't be provided by a human even less after hours of work and fatigue.

There are many technology topics that we could talk about in a casual conversation, and as good as this can be to increase our knowledge, little or nothing changes in the floor until an implementation is completed. Let's start this technology ride, let's review the enablers that will allow you to support your projects. Let's impact manufacturing but above all, let's have fun.

Manufacturing

MANUFACTURING (FROM THE Latin *Manus* –Hand, *Factus* –Make), in its most simplistic definition is the use of human labor and machinery on the transformation of raw materials into a set of finish goods. A Manufacturing Process is the set of steps through which those raw materials are transformed into finish goods.

Manufacturing subscribes to larger concept called Operations Management that deals with the efficient use of the resources and the activities of transformation of raw materials and information into goods (see figure 1). Suppliers provide the necessary inputs while resources within the organization make the expertise and equipment available for the series of tasks responsible of the transformation. This set of tasks is often called production. The output of production is a finish good or a batch of finish goods that is then shipped to the customer. The Operation is a multiple close loop system that receives feedback from the customer on the quality, price and delivery of the goods but also catch opportunities prior to ship the products such as order fulfillment, productivity, Yield and other Key Production Metrics (KPIs). The extent of these multiple feedbacks determines the performance level which is then passed to the suppliers and production. External factors meaning out of the organization such regulations and technology have huge impact in the Operation. The restrictions or rules of the game imposed by the regulatory bodies aim to standardize the best manufacturing practices across the industry and lack of them implies risk beyond potential sanctions. Technology evolves outside the four walls of the factory, the ability to integrate it or not could result in a laggard or in a spearhead efficient operation. The ultimate goal is to transform an operation through the use of technology enablers by infusing them across the different elements of an operation, especially the transformation process.

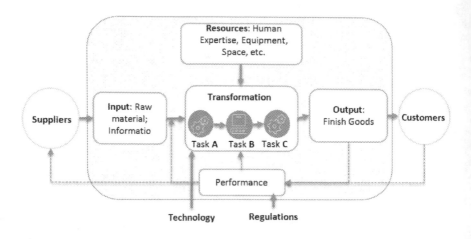

Figure 1 Operations Management

Manufacturing Evolution

Before the industrial Revolution, manufacturing was performed by the artisans, this means all products were made to order and created by hand with huge quantities of human labor and variability. There were not two identical finish goods. This way of making products still exist nowadays and it's called Job Production, where the items are made individually to meet specific requirements like when you make a wedding dress, another example can be a film production or a major construction building.

The industrial revolution dates from 1760 to sometime between 1820 and 1840. One of the biggest transitions of humanity that changed the manual or hand production into a series of processes using machines. Almost all processes were impacted, new business models were created. Mechanical systems were energized or as mentioned by BrynJolfsson and McAfee in the Second Machine Age book [12], humans overcame muscle power limitations, and were able to generate energy at will. This transition took decades with large protest from the Luddites (an English group of textile workers who destroyed weaving machinery as a form of protest), and additional innovations others than the upgraded steam engine.

Moving out of the Industrial Revolution, the mental image of Manufacturing was a cluttered shop floor with large machines and people in greasy overalls working around them. The machine production replaced craftsmanship, and large factories were born. People moved from the fields into the cities and a new social era was born with it. In the 19th century, electricity simplified those large machines and reconfigured the interior of the factories. Now, the machines could be far away from the steam generators without energy losses. The assembly production line made its appearance and was immediately filled with cheap human labor. Later, electricity brought with it a series of innovations that continuously provided productivity increases to this model, the muscle already overpowered by mechanical power energized by steam had a major uplift invigorated by electricity, and the factory as we know it today was born.

Mass production entered in the scene as the preferred way of manufacturing with the aid of electricity, and in early the 20th century, factories became electric and massive, making copies of the best possible product unique configuration dividing the transformation into stations in an assembly line. The factories flows however didn't make sense, the maximum exploitation of the machine was the primary goal, and parts were stocked and moved all around the production floor. By 1920's the influence of Frederick Taylor contributed to synthetize workflows and improve labor efficiency through the application of what is now called scientific management, and by writing his techniques in his book the principles of scientific management [13]. Concepts such as waste elimination, time studies, and standardization were born in this epoch but most importantly, each station can now be approached for efficiency as well as the entire line.

By mid-20th century as written in the Machine that changed the world by James P. Womack [14] a young Japanese Engineer, Eiji Toyoda set out a three month pilgrimage to Ford's rouge plant in Detroit. A plant considered the epitome of mass production, and the most efficient facility of the world. After studying the Rouge plant, Eiji and Taiichi Ohno tried to replicate and improve Rouge model, what Toyota called Toyota Production System (TPS) [15], and ultimately Lean Production.

At this time, with a large influence by the Taylorism, data out of manufacturing was reserved to the engineers, to the only people capable of making sense out of it and providing a diagnosis on a machine malfunction, product quality or a production planning situation. Islands of local information acquisition and processing were born across the manufacturing floor. At that moment, the electro-mechanical power had an ally in the electronic devices that provided a primitive sensing and capacity of processing information giving birth to industrial automation. Workflows were simplified and production lines were revamped with automated solutions to make a single massive, unique, and cheap product over and over again. Productivity gains were shifting from human labor dependent to asset dependent.

It was clear that by the end of the 20th century, the mechanical actions used to transform raw material into finish goods were mastered. A single product could be made in large volumes faster, and cheaper than ever before, by controlling the flow of information using Programmable Logic Controllers (PLC) as the orchestra director instructing machines what to do, and in what order in a simplified automated line.

Before the dawn of the 21st century, information became digital, and the Internet disrupted society creating new business models (and bubbles). "Things" got smarter and mobility entered society connecting the world as never before. Under the pressure of this progress, one fits all products didn't seem appealing, late deliveries were not accepted and having the ability to alter purchase orders at any time was demanded. Manufacturing once again mismatches these new requirements and clashed, still struggling to comply with these new demands.

So now, it is time to Make Manufacturing Cool Again. It is time to give customers what they are asking for. It is time to reinvent manufacturing as we did when moving from steam to electricity, from electricity to automation and now from automation to cyber-physical solutions. It is time to modernize manufacturing by providing high levels of flexibility accompanied by another wave of operating cost reduction, as well as rigorous product quality and worker safety.

The output measure of the impact of this evolution of manufacturing is illustrated by productivity which is the indicator that better captures the success of the manufacturing growth, since its babyhood during the introduction of steam power and electricity, mass production, and Common Sense. Its adolescence during the Taylorism, and its juvenile years exploring the world preaching the Lean concepts, and the early years of automation, or by its entrance to adulthood with process technology enablers such digitalization and Robotization, provided by Industry 4.0. Manufacturing life cycle has been a story to tell full of innovation and continuous search of excellence from the beginning. Figure 2 provides a simplistic view of this "evolution":

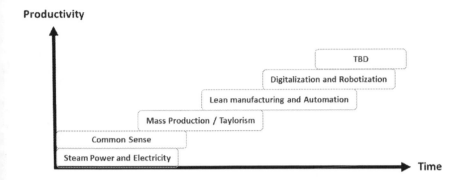

Figure 2 Labor Productivity across
Manufacturing Evolution

Manufacturing has also been influenced by the way society change. Three generations have seen manufacturing drastically change, and have done tremendous contributions leaving huge expectations in the generations to come to reconfigure manufacturing.

Baby Boomers are the post war generation exiting the manufacturing floor and heading towards a well-deserved retirement; under their command, manufacturing continued its productivity positive trend thanks to a mix of muscle, a strict use of Taylor methods and scarce implementations of Toyota Production System.

X-Generations were born reading "the Goal" from Goldratt at school [15], and look at the 401Ks without still thinking about retirement. They inherited a production system and a set of proven tools to continue improving productivity. After TPS got spread in the western hemisphere, the most important accomplishment of Gen-X is the introduction of computer systems into production and the full deployment of Lean principles. They saw the transformation of Japan from being a cheap and low quality producer into a high quality and reliable supplier of goods, so they trust and endorse without hesitation everything related to Lean.

The Millennial generation also known as the Generation Y is marked by an increased use and familiarity with communications, media, and digital technologies. They don't remember Japan unreliable products and don't conceive the job without a computer. They don't understand how China is a communist country and Social Media is part of their daily lives. Their contributions in the manufacturing arena are still to come. However, there's a common denominator they will have to confront and need to master to leave their mark in the production systems universe: The use of disruptive technologies at the floor level on top of the continuous improvement techniques already in place. The way Millennials can clear out the horizon of black clouds of technological ignorance and fears is by preparing to surf the "*technological wave*," is by understanding the elements that constitute what we call the disruptive ideas and technologies.

Having baby boomers in the C-Suite afraid of technology, and blind to the hyper connected world can be a recipe for stagnation. However, having a technology timid leadership as the one represented by Gen X together with a narrow Industrial Engineering thinking will not revitalize productivity either. Millennials have to take leadership and create the change, they need to become technology freaks, create the technology roadmaps to be used by their organizations to reach higher levels of performance. It will be then up to the next generation to formalize and use all the potential of technologies provided by Manufacturing 4.0.

Manufacturing Complexity

The ultimate goal of manufacturing is to deliver high quality products at the right time at the most competitive cost. As a result of social, market, and technological forces, manufacturing complexity is growing. Current manufacturing context is unable to deal with these changes and its inability to deal with this new customer driven new power is creating new winners and losers. So what are these forces, their impact and what solutions we have to deal with complexity?

Social, Market and Technological Forces:

1) **Customization increase**: When the customer can configure his product in a website, his expectation is to receive that precise configuration, any deviation from this expectation means customer dissatisfaction. For the manufacturer, the challenge is how to make at the same or lower cost, and deliver on time this make-to-order product.

2) **Technology**. - The life cycle reduction of the products due to the rapid evolution of key technologies, creates huge expectations at

the customer side. For the manufacturer is a huge challenge to acquire and integrate these technologies into the products and adapt the manufacturing processes. Some businesses are moving into platform solutions that allow the customer to experiment and evolve within the limits of the platform. This means a smooth transition between product generations making manufacturing process alignment less expensive.

3) **Shorten Lead Times**: As a result of the digital transformation the delivery of products and services approach instantaneity. Customers habituated to this type of service wonder why your products aren't in front of their door already, why they can't track their orders. Any deviation of this expectations put loyalty in the sewer. For manufacturers, this situation push them to reduce production lead time, even though most of the waste of time happens in transportation, improve traceability of finish goods, synchronize production with transportation pickups, and intensify visibility of supplier network to reduce risk.

4) **Globalization**: Trade agreements impose restrictions on the amount of material on your product from a certain country or region increasing your supply network. The compliance of the different regulatory frameworks around the world creates encumbrances in your manufacturing that you need to overcome while maintaining the same cost structure.

5) **Markets with specific needs**: Successful products in one region may require revamps to be enticing in other countries or may need to be entirely redesign to be attractive enough to move the customer to purchase it in an emergent country. What works for a culture may not for another and vice-versa. Similarly, some markets are very specific because of an older population or because the level of wealth or because stiffer regulations. Manufacturing needs to produce new configurations at lower cost. This *tropicalization* requires to reduce features of the finish good, align the production system, and revisit the utilization of the capital assets and so on.

6) **Demand volatility**: Due to product customization, technology improvements, and globalization, demand fluctuation is the new constant. A demand driven manufacturing based in make to stock is essentially death, there is too much risk. Manufacturers need to develop supply strategies to minimize inventories but at the transformation process, the alignment requires rapid changes in the setups, minimize the loss of productivity because learning curves, increase visibility in the utilization of capital assets, and so on.

What we can learn from the above forces is that the customer is no longer the passive consumer who use to wait patiently for his goods with low expectations. Customers now are nervously impatient, with large expectations, they are looking for immediacy, impeccable quality, and insanity prices, from companies with high social and environmental awareness. In summary, customers now are cruel dictators ready to swap loyalty at the minimum gap between expectations and product. The impacts on manufacturing processes are bigger than ever, and what is at stake is survival for many companies.

Understand the roots of manufacturing complexity will provide a useful rational framework for improvement. Systems with higher complexity have more problems than systems with lower complexity [20]. So, by having a coherent understanding of manufacturing complexity, we can identify problems in the production system to apply the correct tool, methodology, or technology.

The traditional manufacturing schemes conflict with these inputs (forces), and are unable to respond. The impact is translated into the transformation process with production assets that are barely utilized working at low capacity, longer lead times due to the lack of personnel trained in low volume or rare configurations. The impact is also reflected in a reduction in the quality control levels because the slow adaptation of the inspections, it is also visible in the Overall Equipment Effectiveness (OEE) due to the constant model changes and many others. In summary, manufacturing complexity increases the cost of the overall operation and traditional management tools don't know how to deal with it.

Manufacturing impact:

- **Product complexity.** - It is reflected in the product structure by a larger number of end items or configurations, a larger number of components in the Bill of Materials (BOM) of those end items and the levels in the BOM as well as in the reduction of the commonality between those components. According to Boston Consulting Group, US companies increased year over year new product introductions by 60% between 2000 and 2011 with a meager sales grow of just 2.8%.
- **Data Complexity.** – The above discussed forces increase substantially the size of the volume of data that needs to be handled by the production system as well as the relationship

between data related to the manufacturing of the end goods. There is an explosion of data to the point that now we can analyze the quality behavior of the product, data issued from critical equipment to analyze performance, data from the production lines to track productivity, data from materials on hand for tracking purposes, and inventory optimization, data from training, maintenance, calibration and others to secure compliance, data from suppliers on components to be received in the future, demand data, and so on.

- **Routing Complexity**. - The number of steps in a router contributes to complexity. As the number of steps increases, there are more relationships between the production assets and the components of the bill of materials (BOM). Longer routers imply a larger number of transformation stations or value added points of contact with the product increasing the cost of the operation.

- **Supply Complexity**. - A larger number of components in the BOM indicates a larger number of supplier and a larger pool of suppliers you have, the greater the difficulty to manage them. Even greater if spread around the world. The lack of visibility on these enlarged supply network increases the risk of line downs due to lack of materials, poorer quality and increases in raw material delivery costs.

- **Planning Complexity**. - The ability to route manufacturing flows in real time or change production order priorities electronically at any time creates a domino effect that translates into a production plan change, inventory levels misalignment, materials planning change, etc.

Some companies have launched initiatives to reduce complexity mainly reducing the amount of configurations available by eliminating the low volume products. This rationalization or reduction of the portfolio is accomplished by marketing and passed on manufacturing to execute. This approach not necessarily transfers in a significant reduction of manufacturing complexity.

Balancing the portfolio is essential and important to keep obsoletes and not profitable configurations out of your system, however if no changes to the manufacturing structure are proposed, if *status quo* is the rule to follow then sooner or later the forces above described will catch up on you. Solutions to convert your production system in a more cost competitive, standardized, and flexible system are necessary.

Solutions:

- Lean Manufacturing minimize cost by eliminating waste out of marginal profitable products and creating best practices that dealt with the reduction of manufacturing complexity by enforcing standardization.
- Manufacturing 4.0 provides a set of technology enablers, and innovations that lets a standardized process to handle complexity.

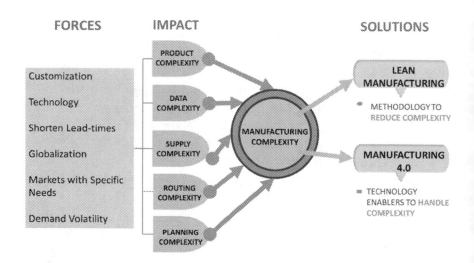

Figure 3 Manufacturing Complexity

The Three Pillars of Manufacturing 4.0

The business models and products under industry 4.0 are interoperable, hyper connected and smart. They use the large pool of data to contextualize and customize solutions. They also use the wave of new technologies coming into maturity to offer platform solutions to increase revenue. Companies as well are hanging onto the industry 4.0 wave by transferring these innovative uses of technology to provide higher levels of profitability, quality, delivery and safety for its workers.

Manufacturing 4.0 is then a subset of industry 4.0 that applies a set of technology enablers to improve manufacturing.

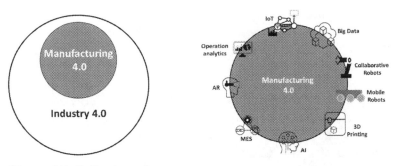

Figure 4 Holistic view of
Manufacturing 4.0

Figure 5 Manufacturing 4.0
Technology Enablers

For a manufacturing process evolving by the introduction of technology enablers, three pillars are considered throughout the book, each of them with a significant impact to tame complexity and create larger pools of profitability: Digital Manufacturing, Robotization or Automated manufacturing and Additive Manufacturing.

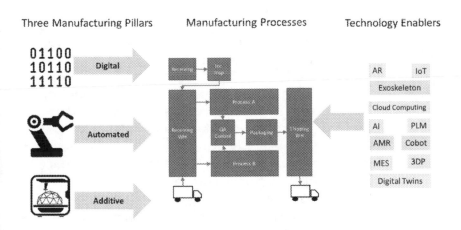

Figure 6 Three pillars of Manufacturing 4.0

Digital Manufacturing uses Information or digital technologies to increase visibility (provides real time data) end-to-end of the supply chain, improves manufacturing to meet consumer demand for speed, value and service and turns to the cloud for agile responses to changing conditions, technologies such as operation analytics, Artificial Intelligence, MES,

Internet of Things, Augmented Reality and others form part of this group. Digital manufacturing allow us to deal with data and product complexity by automating transactions, aggregating data, providing different ways of virtually visualize information, etc.

Automated manufacturing maintains a production floor highly productive with speed, quality and oriented to customer for delivery. Technologies such as Collaborative Robots, exoskeletons and Autonomous Mobile Robots are the line of attack to increase profitability in this group. Automated manufacturing tames routing complexity by reducing human interaction over a larger number of operations. Robots as well, are easier to program and deploy reducing setup times, and increasing re-deployability which consequently increase flexibility.

Additive Manufacturing is a paradigm change that explore vertical integration to reduce supply chain complexity. At the same time, the advantages of building up layer by layer instead of carving out material permits to achieve higher levels of product complexity. Since product complexity is somehow "free" the impact gets reflected in a significant reduction of routing complexity since now less components have to be assembled to complete a final product. The other main advantages from manufacturing perspective is the flexibility of moving from product A to product B effortlessly increasing customization.

Needless to say, all big companies have already started this manufacturing technology expedition. Some have clear strategies while some others have good ideas. But all of them require the support from their leadership. They may call it Smart Manufacturing, Advanced Manufacturing, e-Factory, Factory of the Future, Industry 4.0 or Manufacturing 4.0. It really doesn't matter, at the end they all look for healthier profits, competitive advantage, and a lot of fun. Doing nothing is not an option, leaders must embrace the new paradigm, the rise of the industry 4.0 technologies, and the changes imposed to manufacturing by the market and society forces are real and sooner than later because of the different complexities manufacturing will evolve. The option is to prepare now and start the change creating the necessary strategies or suffer later trying to catch up.

The different expressions of Manufacturing 4.0 offer multiple tangible benefits beyond the traditional functions related to increase of productivity, inventory reductions, and improved quality. In the last chapter of this book, we'll offer our view of the impact of the technology enablers in leadership, environment, and other human disciplines. For now, here is a short list of the impact throughout these business functions:

- **Safety**. - The arriving of manufacturing 4.0 to the manufacturing facility is creating a clash with traditional safety policies due to the higher levels of protection provided by the Collaborative Robots for example. At the same time, connectivity of equipment allow for lockout conditions with higher level of certainty based on inner conditions of the equipment, dangerous zones wirelessly protected for entering by tracking workers. Safety groups are at the center of a storm pushed by the introduction of these technology enablers into the production floor.
- **Environment**. - The potential of manufacturing 4.0 to transform the way companies manage the environmental conditions is huge. Imagine for example component traceability from cradle to grave and the opportunities this brings to recycling! Or all the real time monitoring capabilities for greenhouse emissions, and other energy consuming utilities.
- **Ergonomics**. – In order to maximize comfort and efficiency of the people at work, innovations in Exo-skeletons and other technologies are giving operators better working conditions. The design of workstations is under assault of robotics forcing ergonomics groups to rethink what it means to collaborate with a robot and how this collaboration should take place for example.
- **Training**. - An increase in collaboration is possible thanks to the use of technologies such as augmented reality, and the digitalization of work instructions, manuals, guidelines, and all manufacturing documents.
- **Design**. – Not a lateral function of manufacturing per se but a function residing in the research and development groups that we claim should move beyond those walls to really awaken its potential. It plays a critical role in the organic growth of the companies. The use of technology enablers has been limited to the insertion of a larger number of technology capabilities into the products, however a larger opportunity resides in the thinking of manufacturability 4.0, i.e. develop products that are easier to track by digital tools, products that can talk with the artificial intelligent algorithms used in inspection or other points of the process to transfer its conditions, embedded features in the products to be easily grasped by robots. A rethinking of design manufacturing

golden rules to include the potential of manufacturing 4.0 has to start now.

In the book exponential Manufacturing edited by Deloitte University Press [60] a different perspective of the industry 4.0 technology enablers is presented as cyber-physical solutions. In this context, what the word solution entails is a symbiosis between the digital and physical domains. A solution that goes back and forth taking the best of both:

Physical to Digital. – The purpose is to capture the sea of data from the production floor in order to convert it into digital information. These flows of digital information are then used by software entities to control and improve manufacturing: SCADA, MES, etc. Augmented Reality, for example, allows production crews to combine these two domains in real-time to accelerate learning curves, simplify maintenance or facilitate quality inspections. Now imagine that you scanned your entire factory and have it in your virtual world - you can plan and simulate all your changes without moving a physical asset in the floor. Engineering changes literally took another dimension once you have your digital factory twin.

Digital to Physical. – The purpose is to create algorithms to manipulate information and take decisions that trigger action at the floor level. When you have a 3D model of a component or a fixture, for example, you take that model from your computer to a physical object which eliminates intermediaries, speed up your prototyping cycle, and vertically integrate part of your supply. But above all, it gives you an autonomy that you didn't have before. 3D maps of your factory are used for autonomous robots which optimize routes in real-time and avoid collisions while transporting material for example.

Digital to Digital. - The purpose is to manipulate information to reveal meaning. Using Big Data to unveil mean time between failures in predictive maintenance or using advance analytics to expose non-obvious trends that could cause shortages of material or product delivery issues are examples in this domain.

Whatever the framework is to express manufacturing 4.0, the integration to your operation system of the different enablers is what will result in the desired improvements to the key indicators, and otherwise it will remain as another theoretical background to get to the promise land.

Lean and Manufacturing 4.0 in the
Continuous Improvement Journey

In the Focused Factory Harvard Business review article [7], Wickham Skinner claims that when a conventional factory attempts to do too many conflicting tasks, the result is likely to be noncompetitive because its policies are not focused on the key manufacturing task essential to successfully completing in its industry. He identifies basic changes such focusing the plant on limited, concise, manageable set of products, technologies, volumes and markets. The article written in 1974 still holds good tips and practices for a lot of mass production companies in niche markets and provided the perfect example for the applicability of Lean Manufacturing techniques.

At that time, the world was under transition moving into a globalization adventure, the number of product configurations were limited and the search for cheaper labor was aggressive and ruthless. Manufacturing complexity under the above described scenario meant human variability, trivial knowledge, language barriers, learning curves, non-documented processes. Companies suffering these inconsistencies were desperate for standardization, and ways to find the best known way of transforming raw materials into good products within specifications. It was imperative to be predictable in order to be productive and under this structure continuous improvements was the roadmap in the search for excellence as expressed by Paul Womack in his book Lean Thinking [8].

The history of Lean Manufacturing has its roots in the Just in Time concepts developed by Toyota on its Toyota Production System developed by Taichii Ohno and Shigeo Shingo after the observations and study of the American production and specifically Ford Systems. Lean Manufacturing and its contributions are ubiquitous in the industry. Tools such as Value Stream Mapping, or Japanese concepts such as Kanban, Heijunka, Andon, etc. are common tools as vital as the understanding of the different wastes and the ways to eliminate them. The application of "Lean" has driven productivity increases since the end of the Second World War!

This situation prevailed through the rest of the century with one or couple product configurations made massively, few automations, and the introduction of computer power for production scheduling and to capture some critical data. The Toyota Way became the state of mind with TPS (Toyota Productive System), and the foundations for what it became in

USA the Lean Manufacturing movement as expressed by Jeffrey Liker in the Toyota Way book that dominated the preeminent way of making manufacturing better during the last quarter of the last century until few years ago [9].

Lean as it is better known, continues to be an excellent technique to tame complexity. It has tools and methodologies to rapidly find low hanging fruits to boost your productivity, reduces your working capital, and organize your process better. Simply put, Lean is the right approach when starting the continuous improvement journey, and it should be a predominant way of thinking across your company to remove manufacturing waste.

Manufacturing 4.0 extends the ways by which your production system can continue to bring complexity under control by using process technologies or enablers that empowers your production system to deal with product variants, changes in demand, shorten lead-times and add to the pillars of lean as part of the continuous improvement activities.

In summary, lean and Manufacturing 4.0 aren't contradictory concepts but complementary. The former looks to simplify process complexity while the other one looks to handle complexity. The companies who understand, and apply these concepts as part of CI will undouble higher levels of efficiency. Let's review some of the opportunities of this complementation:

1) Take Manufacturing Execution Systems (MES) for example, one of its core functions is data collection which gathers all the data generated by the production floor. MES compiles large quantities of data that can be harvested for Continuous Improvement purposes. We know that in a discrete manufacturing process, the real cycle times per station is compared against takt time in order to rebalance the line. In the pre-manufacturing 4.0 era, the collection of these data was accomplished using a chronometer or videotaping, exercise that will only provide a snapshot of the process situation at that specific time. Now, automated data collection from equipment, production lines, and others provide larger timeframe visibility, trends for improvement harvesting as well as real time access for decision takers to observe the status of the production floor at anytime, anywhere.

2) One example comes from the robotization. At this moment, industrial robots can't be redeployed easily. They require large

amount of engineering time to reposition a unit or robotic cell. In modern manufacturing, reconfiguring the line for a different product should be nimble, should be an exercise performed by the line assembler in minutes instead of hours. A robot that you can teach the operation by moving its arms and that it can be around the rest of the assembly line operators without being imprisoned in a cage provides the necessary flexibility and re-deployability to have a more agile production system. The new approach is to standardize the operation using Lean techniques, and subsequently look for collaborations between robots and humans to take those activities to higher level of either productivity or quality.

3) Another example is the evolution of the Kanban concept from a system based on physical cards to its digital version giving stakeholders access from anywhere via web. Paper based Kanban was introduced by Taiichi Ohno as a method for Just in Time. The goal of Kanban is to produce only what is required or make to order based on signals (cards) issued by the customer or whoever needs to pull the material. Having a paper card to pass may still work in a small production environments with few materials to replenish, however nowadays the number of materials that need to be handle is much larger, the supply of that material is global geography enlarged to the point that manual Kanban is too slow and cumbersome and became obsolete. It is clear the user advantage of an electronic Kanban but another important factor is that the necessary information to determine the dimensions of a Kanban system are also available online, demand, on-hand inventory, and lead time closing the loop of automation and reducing human intervention. The benefits of Electronic Kanban, online Kanban or Digital Kanban are those to manufacturing by digitalization.

Additional to these examples, there are multiple contributions across the different recognized wastes (TIMWOOD). Here some non-exhaustive simple examples:

Transportation. - The use of Autonomous Mobile Robots (AMR) to reduce transportation. After a Kaizen where you used Job Standardization methodology for the material handling process, you have the routes, dropping points and time schedule for the material delivery. This information is directly converted into parameters to setup the AMR and automate the material delivery process.

Inventory.- There are multiple tools evolving out of manufacturing 4.0 or even before such e-Kanban that reduce the opportunity of making or buying something that will sit in the production lines or warehouse waiting for the next process. Inventory tracking tools that automatically flush the consumed material from the ERP (Enterprise Resource Planning) for example.

Movement. – When the operators and technicians lost time searching for tools, they aren't adding value. Lean movement provided clever ideas like the shadow boards as part of the visual factory. With the addition of Internet of Things (IoT), shared tools can be tracked reducing moving around times. The example of tools can be extended to other critical assets for the operation.

Wait. - An operator waiting is a sign of an unbalanced line. The root causes are multiple, one of the reasons in complex tasks is the slow assimilation of the task or personnel rotation. Augmented Reality provides a mean to delivery instructions directly to the station reducing learning times. Automated data Collection is a mine gold to build the Yamazumi charts used in the balance optimization process.

Overproduction. - This waste is the result of producing more or faster than required. The reasons are multiple, you make more to compensate for losses, long setup times of monuments (equipment), a batch production system, don't trust your forecast, etc. Using AR for TPM (Total Productive Maintenance) helps you to reduce the change overs, Collaborative robots provides you with enough flexibility to move from a job shop type of manufacturing into a cell configuration with flow, and Artificial Intelligence can support your Quality Control efforts to reduce defects to name only a few technologies.

Over processing. - In straight words, over processing is about completing more work than the customer really wants. The root causes once again are varied going from tight tolerances not required, non-standardized working practices that create multiple inefficient ways for assembly or inspection of the materials or goods and others. An immediate typical response is to provide work instructions to the operator, a manufacturing 4.0 response is to provide augmented reality instruction flows to deliver the best known practice. One of the crack of heads for manufacturing is the subjectivity in the inspection process, the answers so far has been over inspection. By introducing AI with machine learning instead of multiplicity of inspections of the same item, the subjective defects are identified reducing inspection total cycle time

Defects. - Scrap costs money and time. The root causes are numerous, from lack of job standardization, inadequate training, lack of skills, incapable suppliers, and so on. Manufacturing 4.0 has solutions for some of the above mentioned causes like AR for training, and limited skills, software platforms to track supplier's quality of raw material even before the physical component makes it to the facility, software for process control that analyses trends, and Cpks, poka-yokes with additional intelligence, and smart vision systems that infer the presence of defects.

In the book Industry 4.0: Managing the Digital Transformation chapter 3, the authors summarize the industry 4.0 technologies and its applicability to the classical type of wastes identified by Lean Manufacturing. We extended the options in the table and provide some examples. See table below:

	IoT	Data Analytics	AR	Cobots	AMRs	Exoskeletons	3DP	AI
Transportation		x	x		x			
Inventory	x	x			x		x	
Motion			x	x		x		
Waiting	x	x			x		x	x
Over processing				x		x	x	
Overproduction	x	x		x			x	
Defects	x	x	x	x		x	x	x

Table 1 TIMWOOD (waste) and
Manufacturing 4.0 technologies

There are direct and indirect effects of these technologies in the reduction of the different wastes. For example, when applying AI to improve predictability of maintenance to reduce the number of times the equipment goes down, then indirectly the time to have the production line back in business is lesser than without it. Similar inferences can be drawn for exoskeletons, for example in operations requiring movement or lifting of heavy objects, an operator wearing an exoskeleton substitutes two operators reducing motion and increasing productivity. Other examples like 3D printing, gives independence to the manufacturer on low volume components and spare parts reducing inventories and by integrating the supply of these components the lead time is close to zero reducing shutdown of lines and consequently waiting time. The grasp of the benefits of most of the technologies is intuitive, and can be deduced with basic understanding of the wastes.

Ultimately, Lean last goal is to add value by understanding what the customer is willing to pay and focusing on those operations by eliminating all others considered as waste. The customer now is changing and demanding more sophisticated products, and shorter delivery times. These demands are creating "fatter" operations because of the inability of those operations to work under this new reality. Therefore, new enablers are required and manufacturing 4.0 provides the technologies and the framework to collaborate with Lean and continue the improvement journey. It is important to note that using the enablers could give you a counterproductive effect if Lean doesn't precede the improvement efforts or used in collaboration.

Manufacturing 4.0 Implementation Strategy

COMPANIES AROUND THE world are realizing that the world is changing, that manufacturing is getting more and more complex and that traditional tools and methodologies are struggling to deal with the new reality even if complete adoption across the organization is prevalent. These companies also realize that a torrent technological innovations is inundating the world and they want to be part of it looking on how to take advantage of it. At the same time, they are aware that customers tend to align with progressive companies that use technology in their products and processes.

To address this challenge a guiding framework is required to take organizations from identifying technological gaps hindering efficiencies to the execution of proposals and projects oriented to transform manufacturing, convert production sites in modern profitable places. A roadmap supporting the strategy is required to align the technologies matching the gaps and have a communication and planning tool.

A three stage model for industry 4.0 is proposed by Semil Erol et al [47]: Envision phase is to comprehend industry 4.0 concepts alignment with company's goals and generate a vision; Enable phase breaks down the long term vision into concrete business model and develop strategies using road-mapping; finally Enact phase transform those strategies into concrete projects.

A developed version to assess for industry 4.0 readiness is the one from Schumacher et al [48] organized in nine dimensions (strategy, leadership, Culture, People, etc.) and three distinct phases: understanding, development and implementation.

The International Labour Organization focus the efforts on a methodology for skills needs with the following steps: Roadmap for smart systems, from which they derive qualitative and quantitative skill needs for organization to analyze social, economic and technological impact and effect [49].

General Electric (GE) has a 5 steps Industrial transformation to become what they call a digital industrial [50]

- Operating Model and Capabilities. - Understand how to configure operations for transformation –determining what capabilities, roles, leaders, and teams are needed
- Data and Connected Infrastructure. - Companies that leverage data and the power of the app economy will set themselves up for long-term success. Schindler uses GE's Predix to reduce unplanned downtime and maintenance costs.
- Partner Ecosystem Pair with partner ecosystems that provide ready-made digital solutions.
- Culture Change. - Transformation doesn't matter unless you've got a culture that's willing and able to embrace it.
- New Business Models. - Creating services opens up the ability for our customers and ecosystem partners to put their own applications, analytics, or micro services all in an effort to accelerate transformation of IT from a cost center to a profit center.

PtC offers the acatech Industry 4.0 Maturity Index [51] which helps companies to determine what stage they are currently at in their transformation into a learning, agile company. The framework is laid in three stages: Analyze current situation and goals, determine capabilities,

1. **Analyze** –company's current situation include what its strategic objectives are for the next few years, what technologies and systems are already implemented and how they operate within the company.
2. **Capabilities** –determine which capabilities the company still needs to acquire in order to successfully introduce Industry 4.0
3. **Roadmap** –This methodology results in the formulation of a digital roadmap for all the relevant areas with a step-by-step approach to achieving the benefits that reduces the investment and implementation risks for the company.

PwC [46] define four value stages on six organizational dimensions: 1) business models and products, 2)market and Customer access, 3) Value chain and processes, 4) IT architecture, 5) compliance, Risk, legal and taxes, and 6) Organization and culture. The four stages for value chain and processes are:

1. **Digital Novice.** – Digitalized and Automated sub process
2. **Vertical Integrator.**- Vertical digitalization and integration of processes and data flows within the company
3. **Horizontal Collaborator.** - Horizontal integration of processes and data flows with customer and external partners. Intensive data use.
4. **Digital Champion.** - Fully integrated partner ecosystem with self-optimized, virtualized processes, decentralized autonomy.

A different proposal with three dimensions: Smart Products and Services, smart business processes and strategy and organization is proposed in the book from Alp Ustundag and Enre Cevikcan [5].

Other maturity industry 4.0 based on the German Standardization roadmap model assess principles such as interoperability, Virtualization, Real Time Data management, Decentralization, agility, across the organization and provides scores on each of these disciplines [52]:

- **Interoperability** means that all CPS (cyber-physical systems) within the plant (workpiece carriers, assembly station, and products) are able to communicate with each other "through open nets and semantic descriptions
- **Virtualization** means that CPS are able to monitor physical processes. These sensors data are linked to virtual plant models and simulation models. Thus, a virtual copy of the physical world is created. In case of failure a human can be notified
- **Decentralization**. The ability of CPS to make decisions on their own and to perform their tasks as autonomous as possible. Only in case of exceptions, interferences, or conflicting goals, tasks are delegated to a higher level. Plant decentralization means that the RFID tags "tell" machines which working steps are necessary.
- **Real-Time Capability** means data is collected and analyzed in real time. The status of the plant is permanently tracked and analyzed. Thus, the plant can react to the failure of a machine and reroute products to another machine.
- **Service Orientation** offers functionalities of all CPS as an encapsulated web service. As a result, the product specific process operation can be composed based on the customer specific requirements provided by the RFID tag for example.
- **Agility** means the flexibility of the system to adapt to changing requirements

Three distinctive phases are common on almost all the above described maturity indexes: 1) A phase to assess the current company's situation against known technologies or capacities related to industry 4.0. At this point, the missing capabilities, and skills are contrasted with the desired state. For example, one method let you recognize how connected, visible, transparent, predictive, or adaptable manufacturing processes are. Another method tells us if our processes are digital novices or digital champions and so on. 2) Next phase outlines initiatives in a roadmap to attain a higher maturity level based on the gaps detected on the previous phase. This mapping is the theoretical framework that will move the needle in one category or another or all. For example, depending on the projects the organization decides to embark on, it can move from being a digital neophyte to a digital champion or moving from being a company with stiff processes to one with highly flexible ones assuming that this transformation will be accompanied with benefits, in the case of manufacturing, of productivity, better quality, safer production systems and shorter delivery times of finish goods. 3) Last phase converts the outlined initiatives into a portfolio of projects ready to be implemented. The ultimate goal for a company is not only to recognize and outline the technologies that will make its operation more nimble, decentralized, real time and interoperable but to transform its manufacturing system. In order to organize the transformation, projects need to be funded, prioritized, executed and track.

Our straightforward high level approach or methodology consist of three stages line up to move manufacturing from the current state to a manufacturing 4.0 state that aligns with the organization goals, the external needs of the market and uses the technological forces driving the industry 4.0 revolution.

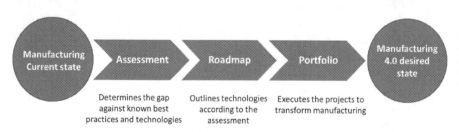

Figure 7 Manufacturing 4.0 holistic approach

Assessment. - The goal of the assessment is not to find technology projects but to determine manufacturing pain points that cannot be addressed effectively with traditional continuous improvement tools. The goal is to exhibit how far the site is from implementing best known manufacturing 4.0 practices.

Roadmap. - The goal is to put in the same plane initiatives that if completed will close the gap between current and desire state. This exercise aims to facilitate planning, provide priority, and align with company and site's objectives. Three important activities need to be accomplish: 1) Outline the technology solutions, 2) Evaluate benefits and risk, and 3) Review with stakeholders and align with organization objectives.

Portfolio. – These are the processes used by the Project Managers (PM) leading the initiatives laid on the roadmap, PM incorporates resources and fine tune priority after developing the business cases that he will use to present to sponsors in order to get funding. Once the projects funded and resourced at the right priority, execution and tracking are the critical activities to complete the transformation.

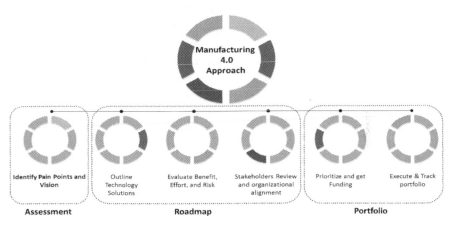

Figure 8 Manufacturing 4.0 breakdown approach

Assessment

In order to facilitate the assessment first and foremost, it is imperative to understand the dimensions we are going to evaluate. Are we going to include all the dimensions in an organization or concentrate the efforts in production related processes only, if so, what functions out of these processes are going to be included? What is the manufacturing vision against which we are going to align the assessment?

The vision of Manufacturing plays an important role at this stage of the overall assessment because allow to calibrate the score. The concept of manufacturing vision ensure that relevant strategic contributions make it to the right priority in the portfolio and that we aren't neglected pain points. Manufacturing vision is in brief the holistic view of how manufacturing will operate in the future. If for example,

A vision then, is an aspirational statement that describes a future state that is intended to serve as a guideline for the course of action. Clarity of the goal even though if aspirational greatly helps to define what a pain point is and where the site is relation to the goal.

For example, a company with a vision of becoming the largest, most profitable, most respected company in the world differs from one which vision is to be the most customer centric company in the world or from another one that wants to utilize the power of Moore's Law to bring smart, connected devices to every person on earth. First one will look to use manufacturing 4.0 as a mean to increase profitability so opportunities oriented to reduce operational cost will be graded higher while in the second case, opportunities impacting customer even slightly will be considered as pain points that need to be solved such as quality and delivery times. In the last case, the use of powerful digital tools for manufacturing will be privileged over other opportunities because it aligns with the vision of the way the company sees manufacturing.

There is no perfect way of doing this exercise, however a candid assessment is the best starting point to identify missing technology enablers and pain points in the manufacturing site. It is normal to overestimate the current state and blindly assign higher scores because either we don't identify the opportunity as important or we don't see in the short term the benefits of the investment. The mechanics of the assessment require the following elements:

- Areas of interest to be assessed;
- Dimensions against which those areas will be evaluated;
- Maturity levels to provides discrimination;
- An aggregation method to create a final score per area of interest for each dimensions

- Visualization and reporting. A simple spider chart to visualize the gaps at each dimensions or each area is necessary as well as a report to compile notes and observations collected during assessment process.
- A questionnaire to guide the process

Areas of interest and dimensions

Performing an assessment to highlight the process technology opportunities related to a specific manufacturing site can be a tricky process when given to the humans as an open book. In order to provide a structure, it is necessary to have a grid summarizing the scores of all the areas for all the dimensions. Another very important aspect of the assessment is to clearly limit the scope of the assessment. As presented along the different chapters of this book, our scope is within the four walls of the factory, even if other inbound or outbound gaps and opportunities are detected, they are not considered here. The dimensions are taken directly from the three pillars of manufacturing 4.0.

The score filled out in the grid for each dimensions for each area at each facility will be the aggregate of result of all the questions asked during the Gemba or walk through of that facility.

Areas of interest	Digitalization (1-5)	Automation (1-5)	Additive (1-5)
Warehouse			
Incoming Inspection			
Quality Control			
Production/Assembly			
Production/Testing			
Maintenance			
Facilities			

Figure 9 Manufacturing 4.0 maturity Score grid

Maturity levels

The maturity level represents a level in the foundation of manufacturing 4.0 in that specific area of interest, so in order to use the same criteria all across, a definition is necessary. This is not a fixed frame but a reference, and multiple score examples can easily be referenced from other methodologies.

Level 1. – Absent. There is zero evidence that even one implementation has been completed in that area of interest or projects in the pipeline, or budget assigned for potential projects.

Level 2. – Initial. Top management identified opportunities on this area, and evidence of some projects in the pipeline are collected, however no project has been completed so far. Basically, there's a recognition of the contribution of the technology in the area but implementation is still at planning stage.

Level 3. - Marginal. Some pilot initiatives as a result of random individual efforts are in progress however no implementation is evident so far. Planning on projects is observed. Basically inconsistent practices and accidental implementations are noticed.

Level 4. - Existent. Scarce implementations as a result of a strategy or planning process are evident. The implementations are validated and the benefits captured and converted into good practices. Required skills are identified, job descriptions adapted to hire ad-hoc talent. Budget is considered for future implementations and a portfolio of projects is active.

Level 5.0- Mature. Evidence of wide spread deployment of technology across the area is noticed. Local experts are available and proactive implementations are palpable. Good practices are documented and processes validated. A robust pipeline of projects to improve the area further are part of the active portfolio.

Aggregation method

The final score or maturity level assigned to each of the areas for each dimension will be the aggregate of all the scores given to the different questions for each dimension. Some areas will contain a larger number of questions than others, so in order to standardize a simple average is proposed for each box of the grid:

$$ML = \frac{\sum_{i=1}^{n} Q_i}{n}$$

- ML= Maturity level
- Q = Question 1 to n

Maintenance	Digitalization (1-5)	Automation (1-5)	Additive (1-5)
Question #1			1
Question #2	3		
Question #3	3		
Question #4		3	
Question #5		1	
Average	3	2	1

Figure 10 Hypothetical Example:
for a Maintenance function

Visualization and Reporting

The aggregated values for each of the areas or dimensions can be visualized with a simple spider chart and the notes collected compiled in a technical report to serve as a baseline.

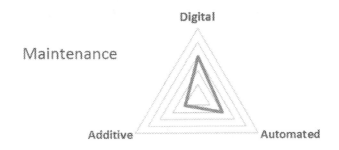

Figure 11 Maturity levels of Manufacturing 4.0 dimensions

Questionnaire

The main tool to perform the assessment is a questionnaire completed during the Gemba. Throughout the walk of the facility a series of questions relevant to unveil the level of maturity in these three dimensions should be asked. Here is short and partial example of a series of questions that you can ask, however we encourage the user to extended it or discard some of them depending of the areas of interest, the manufacturing vision of your company, and above all based on your technical mindset. Not all the questions need to answer to a level of maturity, or be scored, you are free to ask questions to document the way that function operates that will help you to better understand the potential impact of a technology proposal.

Maintenance

1. What happens when nobody in the facilities knows how to fix an equipment? Do you think augmented reality could help you on this cases? Is there evidence of the use of augmented reality (AR) to connect with SMEs to expedite reactive maintenance?
2. Is local maintenance crew using AR technology to reduce learning curves,
3. Do you know about the value of creating a digital twin of a critical asset for maintenance purposes? If so, do you have a digital twin that can be used to monitor maintenance requirements?
4. Are there sensors in place capturing sensitive data from critical components of the equipment?
5. Is there evidence of partial automation of the preventive maintenance? Or 100% of the activities are completed by humans?
6. Is there a machine shop or tooling area? Or do you 3D print spare parts and tooling?
7. What percentage of internally printed or machined parts is versus purchased externally?
8. Do you monitor OEE? Is it manual or automated?
9. Do you display OEE locally? Are the operation stakeholders are using a web base system to visualize this data?
10. Is there evidence of data collection from the equipment to check, running hours prior to next maintenance, and other critical data for the performance of the equipment?
11. Are the maintenance instructions paper base or digital format?
12. Does you maintenance scheduling system send electronic messages or alerts to key stakeholders?

13. Is maintenance planning dynamic? Does it takes into account real time inputs of running hours, production planning, SME recommendations or it is completed by a humans with predetermined fix intervals?
14. Is there evidence of the use of AI or other technologies to promote predictive maintenance?
15. How do you qualify your maintenance by percentage: corrective versus preventive?
16. Is calibration and maintenance consolidated in a single database with the entire list of equipment? If so, how do you ensure that the database is up to date?
17. In summary, what are the main constrains you see in maintenance, and how technology could support you to increase efficiency?

Incoming Inspection

1. Do you have providers supplying electronic data? Do you know if these suppliers have automated data collection capabilities on critical features?
2. Can you connect to their measurement systems?
3. Is there evidence of skip lots, decreased AQL, and elimination of redundant local inspections using supplier data?
4. Do you have CMM, OGP with electronic data transfer capabilities? Are these instruments IoT connected?
5. Do you transfer data out of these (above) equipment somewhere else?
6. What software do you use other than ERP to capture quality data?
7. Is data of the material inspected saved in a digital type of system or transfer to paper?
8. Do you have SPC capabilities at incoming Inspection to monitor quality over time? Is there evidence of analysis of local generated data for statistical purposes in order to prevent issues down the stream due to marginal components?
9. Do you have collaborative robots to feed CMMs, pull testers, or other repetitive measurements?
10. The material samples are transferred in a daily basis from warehouse to incoming by a human or by an autonomous mobile robot?
11. Who determines the priorities of the day, week or month: FIFO, daily planning, other. Is there an automated scheduling system that determines the priority of the incoming material to be inspected?

12. Do you inspect against a quality plan in a procedure, the system or drawing? Are these documents digitalized?

13. What happens with a "bad lot"-what is the flow of activities after rejection? How do you stamp these suspected lot? Do you use an electronic identifier on it to track it and prevent "suspected" material to float around?

14. Do you track the days in hold of the inventory inside the MRB (Material Review Board) cage manually or using ERP transactions?

15. Can you have virtual meetings to gather experts using augmented reality collaborative features in order to discuss MRB material status or to decide to generate RTV (Return to Vendor)?

16. What are the KPI of the area? Do you digital have dashboards to show the KPIs, and display the pipeline of orders (to be inspected), status, and lead time, historic percentage of rejections/acceptance, etc.?

17. How do you coordinate with buyers to create a supplier score? Is this score automatically generated?

18. Do you have critical features that can be inspected by vision systems using neural network algorithms?

19. Are the 3D printed parts inspected against a digital parametric drawing or against a paper drawing?

20. Do you have 3D scanning capabilities? Do you provide digital feedback to the supplier?

21. In summary, what are the main constrains you see in incoming inspection and how technology could support you to increase efficiency?

Warehouse

1. Is there any WMS (warehouse Management Systems) in place?
2. Is there a tool used to facilitate the reception of the material in the system (do you enter the information manually, scan or other)
3. How much material is manually transacted inbound in average per day in number of transactions and volume?
4. Is there a monitoring systems that determines the FIFO of inbound material?
5. How much inventory regularly is waiting to be transacted at the docks?
6. How long does it take to move the material from the docks as received to its warehouse location?

7. Do you transport the incoming material with pallet jacks, forklifts (humans) or with Autonomous Mobile Robots?

8. How the warehouse location is determined? Do you have software support to determine the warehouse location?

9. How long it takes to fill a production order (pick), how it is processed, how many times per day? Is augmented reality an option to improve the pickup process, optimize routes, and confirm pickup locations?

10. The material handler replenish a two bin system or deliver kits, or deliver to a production location in a daily basis? How is this material movement monitored?

11. How many times travels the material handler to the production floor, and what is a typical payload on each trip back and forth? Are AMRs an option to automate this process?

12. What are the KPI that you score and that determines your operational state? Is there a dashboard to show the current performance of the warehouse operation?

13. In summary, what are the main constrains you see in the warehouse operation and how technology could support you to increase efficiency?

Production/Assembly

1. Do you manually collect manufacturing data?

2. Is there MES (Manufacturing Execution Systems in place?

3. Do you have operations where robot-human collaborations are possible?

4. Do you have complex products so opting for delivering Work Instructions with Augmented Reality glasses is a good option?

5. Is turnover an issue so training become an opportunity to use augmented reality?

6. Do you have all your fixtures internally 3D printed?

7. Are you implementing smart poka-yokes?

8. Do you have disconnected processes with material transportation in between that could be a good case for autonomous mobile robots?

9. What is the elapsed time from Production Order generation to the moment the finish goods are transferred to the shipping area? Do you track all the production points to harvest that data for Continuous improvement?

10. When you have multiple configurations to be produced in the same assembly line, how do you handle them? Do you think that a software with Artificial Intelligence capabilities could add value to production planning?

11. Do you have flexible production lines, if so what technologies do you use to reduce the change overs? Do you have AR capabilities installed to expedite this process?

12. Do you have fixed lines (one configuration) if so, did you already made an assessment of the potential of using Collaborative Robots?

13. Do you have cell-stations or areas for subassemblies that feed the line? Do you practice interoperability between these processes, do they communicate or share each other production or product related data?

14. How is the sequencing of the materials throughout the assembly? Do you have visual cues according to the procedure? Is this something you think it could add value?

15. How the material move along a fix production line, manually, conveyor, other? Is there any technology that you have consider to use?

16. Do you have visual cues (red, yellow green lights) in your production material supermarkets to show its state, and autonomously communicate with the warehouse personnel for replenishment or a material handler goes around and check on the min-max levels?

17. How many steps is the longest operation? How long does it take for person to get trained in the assembly of a product? Is AR something that could help to reduce learning curve?

18. Do you share tools between stations? Have you experienced loss of tools or time looking for them? Is tracking using IoT a solution to reduce the time your operations personnel spends looking for tooling?

19. Do you have an up to date VSM with manufacturing technology improvements?

20. Do you have electronic dashboards for your KPI, if so, how do you feed that board, automatically in real time or manually?

21. In summary, what are the main constrains you see in production and how technology could support you to increase efficiency?

Quality Control

1. Do you have all your inspections at the end of your process?

2. Is there any post incoming inspection re-inspection on components prior to assemble them?

3. Do you have inspections with ambiguous criteria?
4. How does the assembly is challenged for lose screws, assembly correctness, etc. are there vision systems or knowledgeable humans checking the assembly prior to final testing?
5. What happens with a part that fails testing?
6. Is there data collection from the testing implemented on the instruments?
7. What are the KPIs that quality control considers successful and how do you monitor them? DPM? FPY?
8. In summary, what are the main constrains you see in Quality and how technology could support you to increase efficiency?

Production/Testing

1. Does your testing is automated or performed manually?
2. Are all the CTQ under test digitalized readily available for consultation?
3. Do you have all your testing stations connected to pull product quality behavior at all times?
4. Are you able to set up alarms on the testing whenever there is an error in the sequence?
5. Are your testing operations automatically reconfigured based on product configurations or manually reconfigured consuming time and prone to error?
6. How do you validate or revalidate the testing stations? Are you allowed to use historical data and if so do you have it?
7. Is maintenance and calibration of your testing stations automatically checked for each production run?
8. If testing/inspection shows subjectivity are you willing to use AI algorithms and trust the results without confirming them by a human?
9. Are the data collected from the testing automatically added to the manufacturing report?
10. In summary, what are the main constrains you see in Testing and how technology could support you to increase efficiency?

Facilities

1. Do you have all your critical assets connected to an IoT network: HVACs, sensors, lighting, filter systems, etc?
2. Can you turn on and off assets remotely?
3. Do you or your facilities crew receive alarms and remote access to the facility assets whenever a crisis occur?

4. Is the business continuity plan considering technologies to palliate risk?
5. Do you surveille premises with drones?
6. Is there data available to check on energy consumption?
7. Do you receive seismologic information in your mobile?
8. Do you use simulation software to optimize pressures and flows in controlled production environments: Cleanrooms?
9. Do you consider active or passive exo-skeletons for workers dealing with movement of heavy equipment?
10. In summary, what are the main constrains you see in facilities and how technology could support you to increase efficiency?

NPI

1. Do you support your actives using a PLM (Product Life Management) software?
2. Do you use process optimization digital tools prior to deliver layout and process documents to production?
3. Do you have 3DP capabilities to optimize fixtures?
4. What is the regular lead time to introduce a new product, how do you track it and harvest it for improvements?
5. What are the main challenges from production perspective? Do you deliver 100% digital documentation: Drawings, procedures, quality plans, etc.?
6. How do you train production on new products and processes? Do you use AR to reduce learning curve or reaffirm learning process?
7. In summary, what are the main constrains you see in NPI, and how technology could support you to increase efficiency?

Roadmaping

There are many different type of roadmaps, but all seek to answer three fundamental questions [62]: 1) where do we want to go? 2) Where are we now? 3) How can we get there? The purpose is to put in order the right manufacturing technology required to achieve future higher levels of efficiency.

Outline Technology Solutions

Roadmaping is the tool that will outline the manufacturing technology solutions over time. The verbiage of the potential solution to a pain point detected during the assessment requires a translation into business goal, we will check that what we are considering a pain has alignment with the business, and we will need a clear operational problem description to check that we are proposing a solution to an operational problem and that we are able to express it in production, quality, maintenance, etc. terms. Finally, we will propose a technology that we consider will solve that operational problem. It is important to highlight that we are not demanding a specific technology for that solution but a proposal.

Example #1: Automated Data Collection for Critical Equipment

Business Goal	Problem in Production	Technology proposed
Agility and responsiveness	• No visibility on OEE, and Production information • No real time KPI tracking • Stakeholders not in the production site 100% of the time • Inability to analyze production data	• Web based Platform for data acquisition to connect PLCs, HMIs, and other process controls. • OPC and LAN Network • Software Development

Example #2: Collaborative Robots for Loading and Unloading

Business Goal	Problem in Production	Technology proposed
Maximize Productivity and efficiency	• Repetitive Manual loading and unloading at equipment XYZ	• Collaborative Robots (UR3) from Universal Robots • Special 3 finger gripper • Laser Radar (LIDAR)

Example #3: e-DHR Implementation

Business Goal	Problem in Production	Technology proposed
Increase compliance	Manual Device History Records (DHR) generate multiple data entry errors for training, maintenance, calibration, line clearance.	• MES Software Platform • Scanners • Thin terminals • RFID

Example #4: Warehouse-Production Material Movement Automation

Business Goal	Problem in Production	Technology proposed
Decrease operating cost and reduce inventory in transit	• Material handling hours consumption (waste) • Delivery subject to personnel availability	• AMR • Laser Scanner • AMR Software Platform • Sensors around facility

Example #5: Exo-skeletons for heavy lifting

Business Goal	Problem in Production	Technology proposed
Improve ergonomic conditions	• Several operations require the lifting of heavy components • Two hours rotation	• Passive exo-skeletons

Example #6: Very Low Volume 3DP components supply

Business Goal	Problem in Production	Technology proposed
Improve COGS	• Line shutdowns for lack of material • Long lead time on rare components • Premium payments	• SLA 3DP

Evaluate Impact and Effort

Once the business goals, problem definition and technology proposals are articulated for each of the pain points, these technology solutions are evaluated in terms of direct benefits, risk and effort for that specific site. The positive impact or benefit can be tangible financial benefits, ergonomic improvements, better safety conditions, higher quality, and shorter delivery times. The risk associated with implementation are associated with the lack of skillful resources to complete, maintain and improve the technology during and after installation or cybersecurity threats that could result in disruption to production.

The bubble graph plots the magnitude of the projected effort and the benefit in order to visualize it against the other technology proposals. There is a level of subjectivity on the analysis, because it is a simple matrix to help you to situate each project in a quadrant for a visual analysis. Once your proposal is in a quadrant you determine the level of risk by the size of the bubble. There are no rules on the plotting of these three elements, you can plot risk and effort and make the size of the bubble for the impact, etc.

In the case of the examples exposed in the previous section, the magnitude of the effort is higher for an implementation of an MES solution than for the installation and qualification of a set of collaborative robots and it differs from the installation of a plug and play data collection system. In regards to the risk, MES is exposed to regulatory bodies and FDA (Federal Drug Administration) audits so it requires a flawless implementation since any slip will have a large repercussion. A collaborative Robot has a risk associated as well that requires to be evaluated in a risk analysis prior to the implementation, is the unit going to be in a zone with dense human traffic? Are there production associates entering the robot field of action to interact with it?, are common evaluation questions of this risk assessment. An AMR is not free of risk as well, you can encounter a unit in the middle of the production area without battery causing a further problem. The benefit as mentioned above, doesn't necessarily need to be exclusively in financial since a good ROI (Return on Investment) could be accompanied by a large level of dissatisfaction impacting turnover creating a problem where there was none. Thus, taking into account the four examples and their plotting.

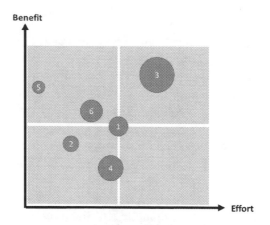

Figure 12 Technology Proposal Plotting

Stakeholders Review (Prioritization)

Once the session of benefit and effort is completed, it does not mean that all proposals can be implemented at once. At this moment, the business goals are equalized, i.e. we don't know the priority for the organization of a large effort, with great benefits and medium risk MES implementation versus a low hanging fruit proposal to implement collaborative robots to increase productivity in a specific product line. The other factor to bear in mind while doing the prioritization is the level of maturity of the different departments. There is no reason to have all the operational functions digitalized or automated, so we may want to prioritize that area before the others, or shift similar projects for the different functions over time, etc. The result of this prioritization will be the ordered in time of the different proposals. The timeframe to consider depends on the level of urgency the specific site and the investment the organization is willing to put into the following fiscal years budgets.

Many stakeholders are involved in the development, implementation, support and use of the roadmap. Thus, the scheduling is an exercise to be completed by and for the stakeholders, and translated into the goals and objectives of the different leaders of the organization to be assessed as part of their personal and organizational performance. The decisions taken during the exercise since subjected to uncertainties associated with the future of the operation need to be revisited in a frequent basis. A roadmap can be as simple or complex as the different participants define it, a simple example is shown below:

Fiscal Year	1	2	3	4	5
Digital	Automated Data Collection for Critical Equipment	e-DHR Implementation		Warehouse Management System deployment	AI assistance for inspection operations reduction
	Real time production dashboards		AR for occasional product configurations		Digital Twins for all critical equipment
Automated	Collaborative Robots for Loading Equipment	Exo-skeletons for heavy lifting operations	Warehouse-Production Material Movement Automation		
	Collaborative Robots to complete the palletization	Exo-skeletons in the warehouse		AMRs for production to shipping	
Additive	3DP fixture capabilities	Low volume 3DP supply		Mid volume configurations 3DP supply	
	3DP for spare parts				

Figure 13 Manufacturing 4.0 Roadmap for facility XYZ

Portfolio

The Program Management Institute (PMI) defines a portfolio as a set of projects, programs or other portfolios containing other programs and/or projects. Since our interest is on the management of the technology proposals outlined, prioritized and scheduled in the roadmap, we'll simplify the entire portfolio as a set of digitalization, automation and additive programs each of them containing a group of projects. In order to move from potential to active project, a more detail review of proposal is required for the sponsors to approve and stakeholders to calibrate expectations. These are the elements that such a charter could include: Project Title, Leader, Team Member, Sponsor, Strategic alignment, Objective, Benefits (Safety, Quality, Delivery, Cost) explanation, Description of the future state, financials breakdown, diagram or sketch, in and out of scope, potential issues and risk, start and end date. The roadmap is a great tool to plan the investments and complete the budget exercise year over year.

The management of the portfolio varies from company to company and the goal of this book is not to provide program management recommendations but to highlight the importance of execution to collect the benefits of manufacturing 4.0 technology proposals.

Digital Manufacturing - *Digitalization*

THE BUSINESS MODELS that digitalization has transformed are innumerable, industries untouched by the digitalization wave maybe rare or in via of extinction. The examples are abundant like having the opportunity to interact with your house, make a payment without going to the bank, read a book a second after it was published, interact with friends, book a room to stay in a city, use the telephone to board into a plane, and so on. When IBM helps to protect endangered species by installing them IoT sensors connected to the cloud to protect them from poachers that's when we realize that the digitalization of the world has no reverse.

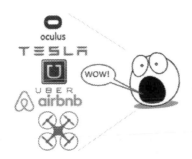

In the innovation clash provoked by the digitalization of the world, there is an embedded change on the way we understand the world around us, the way we use and enjoy technologies when they become affordable but what are these technologies already influencing how people behave, and how the world is changing? Here are some simple examples that will support the fact that digitalization is sweeping all type of business models, all market segments, and all society elements:

1. The decay of the Combustion Engine. - For all those who had a dream of having a rumbling car, the only noisy element in today's electric cars is the driver. This technology which dates from 1859 and that has mediocre energy efficiency limited by the Carnot cycle is polluting the air with Carbon Monoxide and Nitrogen Oxides, that is why is one of the favorites to be replaced. Even though Silicon Valley and Detroit with their large pockets and appetite are aggressively moving into the electrical car direction, there is still years ahead to see the fossil fuel pump stations out of business. The cars are now well known as computers on wheels completely digitalized from the steering of the wheel, the brakes, energy consumption, and so on.

2. The Virtual Reality rides. - Fun, fun, fun. Imagine you are flying across buildings being attacked by creatures but instead of having all the experience through your eyes using a headset, you are in a roller coaster! Whoever put these two experiences together is a genius. I can only see more and more amusement parks integrating these technologies and igniting creativity. Your ride will be different every time. The creation of these virtual worlds only exist in a digital form.

3. The extinction of the Taxis. - The time will come when you will answer the question, what is a taxicab. Memories and images will fly to your head immediately replaced by the words Uber or Lyft. These companies not only disrupted the way we transport ourselves, destroying unions on their way but they are also changing the way we think about employment. There are good and bad on the approach of these companies but one thing is sure, there is no way back. The digitalization of the commuting activity is a reality.

4. No more park meters. - I was astonished when my daughter explained me how to use the Parkmobile app. I did like it immediately. Imagine that you are in the middle of your movie or dinner and you have to go out to put more coins to the park-meter! Not anymore, you continue enjoying your evening by adding parking time using your mobile. Kuddos to whoever thought and made this come true.

5. Drone me. - It will mean send me something using a drone; it could be information coming out of the activity the drone is doing –spying your neighbor, photo-shooting, collecting traffic or weather information or a shipment if you provide your GPS location. Today, drones are used mostly in Military, virtual races and entertainment in general, but there are some other very important applications such as detecting landmines and we are certain that this is only the tip of the iceberg.

6. No rooms available. - Airbnb is not only reshaping the relationship between host and guest. It is also opening alternative revenues for people other than big chain hotel owners. It is charming when you stay closer to the real people, the real place that you are visiting and even more when it is cheaper than a luxury hotel. These two models continue fighting and the way they will cohabit in the future is still uncertain.

7. No more paper boarding passes. - As incredible as it looks, you can still see couple people boarding airplanes with papers in hand.

Nowadays, majority of people use their phone. There are some advantages on checking in with your mobile: you do not need to look for a printer or get 10 minutes before to the airport to print your pass; you can receive updates and know the gate of departure, etc. This is a technology that is becoming widespread and probably we won't' see Kiosks in the airports in the near future.

There are many other very important innovations on multiple business segments revolutionizing the world such as Genomics, Artificial Intelligence, and big data. While the above set of examples are by no means all-inclusive, they are however, a list of popular business models, easy to grasp and understand that I hope will be your initiation to the digitalization of the world you will share with your kids and grandkids.

In this section, the term digitalization is used instead of digitization as the use of digital technologies to provide value-producing opportunities as described by the IT Gartner dictionary. Digitalization have computer power, software and connectivity at its core.

In this section as well, we are going to review the different technologies that reached maturity to make digital manufacturing possible. We'll also review, how to harness the digital power in order to create digital twins of critical assets, IoT applications, and augmented reality uses, artificial intelligence algorithms to improve the planning process, subjective inspections and other. In short, how to unveil the power of a digital manufacturing to impact safety, Quality, Delivery and Cost.

Digital technologies aren't new in manufacturing, predominantly at design phase. Computer Aid Design (CAD) are one of the oldest applications that moved from 2D to 3D parametric modeling with the support of storage capabilities and processing power. Finite Elements simulations are now a common feature on design software packages. The statistical process control, long time ago performed by humans and charts is all digitalized now and it takes a snap of the fingers to have trends, analysis to take decisions on the process under surveillance. Based on the constant increase of computational power driven by Moore's law, the type of applications of computers in manufacturing were vastly deployed for pre-production activities such as design and simulation. CAD that at the beginning was cumbersome to use, went through a series of improvements that made it a must have for any manufacturing site instead of a nice to have. CAD systems are now indispensable for manufacturing because of the integration they have with machines in charge of parts production. Now, you send the parametric file directly to a CNC (Computer Numerical Control) machine or a three dimensional printer. CAD files are used for layout purposes that feed process optimization software used to improve material movement or process design. One constant on the use of digital tools (computers), at this point computers were mainly used to encapsulate engineering knowledge related to design of new products or process. Direct increases in productivity weren't evident, as affirmed by Solow's paradox: *You can see the computer age everywhere but in the productivity statistics.* Economist Robert Solow said that productivity growth lagged in the 1970s and 1980s despite the computing revolution [59].

The other big area within manufacturing where computers found a perfect application is Enterprise Resource planning (ERP). These are systems used to integrate all data and processes of an organization into a unified system from resources planning, financial accounting, and business processes of the entire enterprise, including areas such as human resources, project management, product design, materials and capacity planning [60].

Simulation, design, statistical control or ERP implementations are all digital to digital applications, meaning that a digital input is received or converted to digital after a manual entry and the result is a digital output in the form either as a finite element analysis, digital information from the ERP system or a parametric version of a digital product from a CAD software. In other words, the automation of manufacturing information by the use of computers! Great as it is for planning or for fine tuning a new product, few or no impact in the physical transformation of a raw material to convert it into a finish good is done by these applications. Few applications deployed in the production floor were available. It is until software was mature enough, process technologies grew exponentially, storage became cheap, and other technologies were available that:

- Digital work instructions can be deployed with the most immediate information reducing the impact of lagging engineering changes or updates in revisions
- Manufacturing Execution System (MES), and MOMs (Manufacturing Operations Management) were trustable enough to provide real time information about jobs and orders, labor and materials, machine status and product shipments.

- The introduction of sensing technology combined with larger bandwidth and standard communication protocols resulted in the boom of Internet of Things and all the range of applications for manufacturing
- The Virtual Reality became a factor of influence for the design of production sites, laboratories or to assess the interaction of the consumer with the product.
- Augmented Reality impacted productivity by reducing the learning curve of new products, increase collaboration between functions of operations, and provide tools for maintenance crews to resolve technical problems faster.
- Real time production dashboards are ubiquitous reducing all the manual entries, and waste of personnel in non-value added activities.
- Artificial Intelligence engines can be applied for subjective quality inspections or for scheduling and planning.
- It is possible to track all the components of a product and the product itself from supplier to the customer, or have a digital footprint of the quality behavior of all the components included in the final product.

The evolution of digital manufacturing goes beyond the four walls of the factory and the number of applications is growing exponentially that is difficult to categorize them. In an attempt to show light to this digital revolution in the production floor, a series of basic technologies are shown aiming to sample the wide range of digital manufacturing power and possibilities.

The first case will be a series of tools to improve efficiencies around a workstation such as real time monitoring dashboards, digital tools to secure that the most recent work instructions are used for the current production order, and other tools to check on the quality of the product. For the sake of a better term, we'll call this group Digital Manufacturing Monitoring and operation analytics. The benefits are in most of the cases to have the most recent information available to modify behaviors in the production floor.

The second case of digital manufacturing is made for the Internet of Things (IoT) and the tsunami of applications derived from this concept that gathers different technologies and that is having a huge impact in manufacturing.

The third case we make is for Manufacturing Execution Systems, the Digital movement in manufacturing is consolidating a concept that dates from the beginnings of digitalization but that now materialize thanks to the progress in connectivity and better integration with ERP systems.

A nascent set of applications are using the power of big data to feed machine learning algorithms with impact in different manufacturing functions. A fourth case, will be shown the power of AI in manufacturing.

The fifth case is for digital twin, these digital duplications, and their use for product and process optimization are analyzed for manufacturing, as well as how these twins can be used for predictive maintenance and other functions.

Finally, the sixth case is for the extensive set of applications around virtual and augmented reality, the impact on maintenance and production are major and an open market with very creative solutions is growing rapidly.

The common denominator of the above described digital technologies is that all of them materialize in the production floor and its impact is reflected in metrics affecting the day to day operation. There are certainly proven digital applications impacting other areas and functions of manufacturing such the use of the digital power to design, analyze and optimize an entire factory by creating a digital twin of it that can easily be transferred to a different location with the correct assets, or the extensive number of digital tools oriented to improve customer satisfaction by tracking purchase orders in real time, and by providing a digital history of the purchased product in terms of quality, or the tools used to allow the customer to be part of the innovation process of the new generation of products, or the set of precursor software for simulation and product design even though we don't deny the large contribution of all these technologies, the emphasis is given to the four walls of the factory, the illustration below shows a graphic representation of the tools of this section.

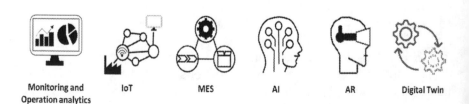

| Monitoring and Operation analytics | IoT | MES | AI | AR | Digital Twin |

Figure 14 Digital Manufacturing Tools

Digital Manufacturing Analytics and Monitoring

Manufacturing Monitoring

The collection of data from the production floor can be used for visualization and monitoring purposes or for further analysis to induce decisions from it. By displaying data in specific context and format in a dashboard, we expect the observer of the displayed data now transformed into information to take action based on what is happening or on why did it happen. Collecting and monitoring data plays a key role in the Visual Factory.

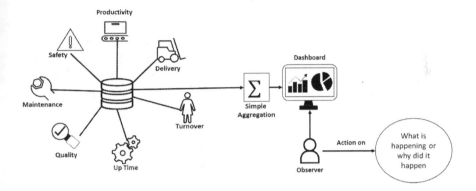

Figure 15 Manufacturing Monitoring

Dashboards to monitor the operation are not a new concept. They provide a quick overview on high level measures of performance. Dashboards to track the Key Process Indicators are not the only type of dashboards in manufacturing either. There are strategic boards for leaders to check on business opportunities, or simple informational boards used to display organizational, or company related information. A dashboard has to be simple and communicate easy with the rest of the organization, it is important to display relevant information instead of cluttering the board with redundant, not prone to action information.

The concept of tracking productivity in a board belongs to the use of visual controls so no problems are hidden as described by the TPS (Toyota Production System). Management thinker Peter Druker often quoted for saying that you can't manage what you can't measure offers a simple reason why having a performance board is useful, the way you realize if you are successful is by defining how success looks like and tracking it. Thus, there is no better way to check the level of success than displaying it for everybody involved in production to realize the current performance state.

Dashboards are rarely manual nowadays, they are devices displaying information coming from a software platform that aggregates the information from multiple sources. A digital dashboard is a tool that helps to increase the visibility of what happens in the production floor. The channeling of the information to the final visualization device could be as simple as streaming static information from a power point file or from any other software package via HDMI, Wi-Fi, Bluetooth or other type of connectivity. However, the value of this is limited and is frequently used for informational boards only. The possibility of streaming data from multiple sources opens the door to capture dynamically the status of production, in other words, take the pulse of production in close to real time intervals. At the same time that aggregation of these multiple sources becomes a reality, the way we display information has diversified as well. The channels that we can use to display are not only TV monitors but any visualization device connected to Internet, adding a factor of mobility by using mobile phones and tablets. In this sense, digitalization added new functions to dashboards as well as a new adjectives:

- **Interactive**. - The information displayed can be manipulated by the visualization devices to show different timeframes, or a different mix of KPIs, or simple different formats and colors that change depending on the value below or above certain threshold. The possibility of playing with the way the information is displayed provides a different perspective to the analysis and potentially a different decision or action.
- **Historical**. - A computer compiled the information from different sources and stream into the display, however these data is also stored in a database. Storing the data allows to consult the database to aggregate data and show it as trends or simply display it at different timeframes
- **Mobile**. - Doesn't matter where you are, if you can connect to the network you can see the dashboards of the site you are responsible of.
- **Real time**. - Immediacy of the information is crucial when dealing with decisions that impact human's safety, product quality, delays of shipments, and cost of production.

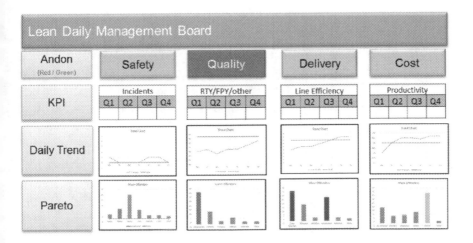

Figure 16 Digital Dashboard example

Manufacturing Analytics

When manufacturing data is analyzed, we are able to predict what is likely to happen and take a decision on what should be done about it. After collecting the data we have the option to report it directly into a dashboard or send it to a gray box for data mining, interpretation, and communication of meaningful patterns in data.

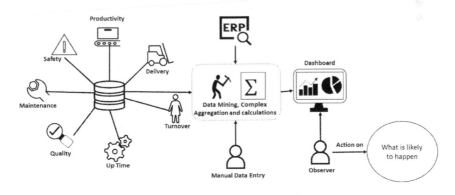

Figure 17 Operation Analytics

Manufacturing analytics goal is the analysis of the collected data to automatically identify areas of improvement. For example, collecting data of uptime for a machine and combing that data with the minimum and maximum cycle times achieved historically for a specific configuration can provide a better prognosis if the production plan of the day will be achieved or not. In quality, collecting scrap codes data directly from the equipment performing the inspection operation gives the opportunity to identify patterns for different configurations, or shifts, seasons of the year, etc. This capacity goes beyond of simply displaying a Pareto chart of the defects in a dashboard and let the stakeholder to take an action. It provides a second level of information allowing to target specific areas of the manufacturing system to solve problems and improve efficiencies. Patterns of turnover spikes can be associated to social events in the city where the plant is located or weather conditions. The data is transformed into knowledge and presented to the user to determine what is likely to happen based on the data.

Manufacturing analytics is only possible thanks to the recognition of manufacturers of the power of data, however other factors have influenced its growing applications: the cheaper processing power, the lower cost of storing of data, the spread of bandwidth, and the ubiquitous use of computers in manufacturing.

Internet of Things

Kevin Ashton who in 1999 coined the term Internet of the Things [56], meant using the Internet to empower computers to sense the world for themselves. It happens that now computers are everywhere, you can find a computer in a telephone, washing machines, production machine, cars are computers in wheels, etc.

Having high speed processing computers sensing the environment connected through the internet triggers a lot of new business models, and a boom of new potential applications, it opens the door to use "things" as an extension of human capabilities. Primitive capabilities of sensing are now attributed to devices, machines, and things. Flows of data acquired from these devices are connected to other devices through the biggest network in the world, creating the internet of things. Such interconnectivity doesn't stop to grow as new devices with IoT capabilities land into the market. Even though the adjective smart is now commonly used to any devices with IoT capabilities, it seems more adequate to simply call that device connected. The contextualization and further processing to enrich the collected data for humans to take decisions, or for other devices to trigger actions based on the digested information is what drives value when applying IoT, if no value is added after transmission of the data, then it is simply another connected device. The value of IoT falls into diverse market segments: House, Cars, offices, wearables, Cities, transportation, retail, etc. however the opportunities can be classified between those transforming the way you operate, the way your processes function oriented to improve profitability, and those enabling new business models to increase revenue. In Manufacturing, even though we care about the top line of a Profit and Loss statement, we care more about the type of opportunities that can make our transformation process more efficient. In this scenario, IoT is applied to connect equipment, devices and processes to improve asset utilization, increase productivity, provide predictive maintenance, surveille quality behavior of product along the production process, etc.

All IoT applications follow a sequence of sensing (data collection), transmission (Internet), and aggregate of data coming from different sensors at different devices (software platform) to analyze them either by a human or an artificial intelligence agent. The result is an action that change the behavior of the device under surveillance. This cycle is defined by Deloitte [57] as the information value loop and explains at each step the infrastructure, and tools applied that makes IoT a powerful technology.

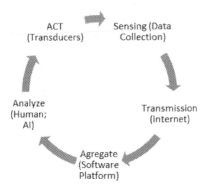

Figure 18 IoT Applications Cycle

The common example is the thermostat in the house sensing local temperature that transfers its signal through Internet to another device (your smartphone), the phone device aggregates information from the thermostat with weather forecast, and display it for you to act by taking a decision on turning the A/C on now, or in 20 minutes, etc. This automation process cycle takes care of your house temperature conditions regardless of your physical location. Other applications on this sense-act scheme are mostly house applications such smart plugs that monitors how much energy your devices are using, helping you to make your home more energy efficient; connected bulbs that you can turn off and on from your phone; locking systems that unlock automatically when you are at home and locks behind you when you close the door, systems that send you video of the front door activity when someone approaches or ring the bell giving you extended capabilities of communication and interaction; pet feeders that monitors your pets food consumption even when you are away from home.

Another way of looking at this process is the DIKW hierarchy, or pyramid as it is known (see figure below).

Figure 19 DIKW Pyramid

Real time data is collected from PLCs or sensors connected to the "thing" that it can be a sophisticated automated equipment, an instrument in the production floor, a product traveling across its manufacturing process, a critical tool, etc. Data is contextualized, and becomes information, for example vibration is over the limits, current drawn is normal, or location information is translated into local building names and so on. The information is analyzed to generate knowledge, for example, based on the fact that vibration is over the limits, the wear off of the bearing maybe compromised, since the electronic current is normal there's no over torque conditions, Building A is located 800 feet from your current location, etc. That knowledge then is use it to improve the conditions of the "thing", in other words, to optimize it, so we act; we change the parameters or launch a maintenance routine, or generate a route in the map to locate the lost asset, etc.

IoT Components

IoT applications cycle require at least three fundamental elements for functioning. At the front edge, it requires of sensors and actuators to acquire data and control the "thing." In the transmission layer, it requires a connectivity technology to transport the data towards the software platform for the data to be aggregated somehow.

IoT Applications in Manufacturing

The impact of IoT across manufacturing is ample and it has different segments or areas of applicability, connected factory, Facility Management, asset management, predictive maintenance, IoT instruments, production monitoring, safety and more. Here are some examples:

Digitally Connected Factory

As manufacturing complexity goes up, the ability to have an efficient production system using traditional methods gets more complicated. The reason as explained in previous chapters is the amount of variations in the features of the goods, the steps in the routing, and the supply of the components and so on. The data produced by those variations impact the number of adjustments made to the equipment, the number of assembly instructions, etc. Performance optimization comes from the digital connectivity of the production assets, its monitoring, planning and visibility using IoT to reduce change over times, create real time productivity dashboards, help to plan production based on real time efficiency data, etc. These applications even if straightforward on the collection from the production floor and its utilization for production optimization are considered IoT applications because all of them follow the DIKW hierarchy and use Internet as framework for communication. For example, taking data out of a working station for calibration, directly from the equipment or through a scanning, provides the data flow, that data contains contextual information related to the date, hour and type of equipment prior to be communicated through the local network to a software such MES or other to aggregate the data where it can be compared to issue a within or out of calibration statement for the specific asset. The same cycle can be simulated for the automated adjustments of an equipment based on specific configuration of the product under production. Future applications for interoperability relays in the capacity of a production asset to talk to the asset next in the routing to provide critical information about the product being transformed, its own running rate to improve planning, an optimize flow, eliminate waste and avoid unnecessary work in process inventory.

Facility Management

The amount of data coming from systems in buildings is ramping up, the ability to convert such data into useful information provides an advantage in terms of cost reduction and business continuity. The biggest example are HVAC systems connected for monitoring purposes, and controlled based on the number of associates of production in an area. The entrance gate counts the number of people in an area and transmits the information to the management asset software, which aggregates that information with temperature sensors directly from the area and determines the HVAC parameters in real time. The impact on cleanrooms used in the medical device industry is even larger due to the requirement of particles per unit of space that need to maintain and because humans are the number one carrier of dust, particles and others. The energy consumption, waste disposal and others have also a large impact because of the capability of remotely and automatically manage related equipment by setting the parameters to save energy and cost.

Asset Management

Asset management is the process of keeping track of your company's assets and their information along the supply chain. In our case, well restrict to the management to the assets in the four walls of the manufacturing facility. The way most operations run is by trusting its associates of the location, correct use, notifications, and history of use, however this trust erodes when turnover is high and the number of assets is too large to keep track manually. How much time do you spend searching for assets around the facility? At least half an hour or more searching equipment, tools, and products was the answer from attendees of an Ubisense webinar.

Implementing an asset management solution implies tagging the assets and manage them using a management software. IoT tracking technologies vastly reduce human effort – and error. RFID, BLE and GPS technologies are used to read multiple tags for workers to accurately locate assets.

Manual:
- Loss of production time
- Loss of assets
- Underutilization of assets
- Loss of critical information
- Inaccurate asset physical inventory

IoT enabled:
- True cost control
- Asset reporting
- Asset life cycle management
- Critical information protection
- Real time physical inventory

Figure 20 Manual and IoT enabled Asset Management

In general the benefits of implementing an IoT asset management solution go beyond supporting production shadow boards. It provides extended analytics, real time alerts, and reporting capabilities beyond of the location of assets for example:

- Improves asset safe keeping by preventing the asset from be out of premises or designated areas.
- It provides maintenance alerts to better schedule maintenance and calibration of asset diminishing the production line interruptions.
- When critical production assets are located quickly, productivity increases inevitably
- The natural response when assets aren't located is to purchase extras (if low capital assets) and inundate the production floor of redundant capacity converting asset inventory in a guessing game and missing a true cost control.
- Achieve real-time physical inventory of assets
- Knowing where the assets are provides timely information for decision making related to purchasing, inventory and production.
- Having the usage information allow to track the number of hours the asset will stay perform as intended or until it requires replacement providing cost predictability.

IoT is reshaping human-asset interaction in an incredible way. Companies offering solutions are countless, it suffices to search in Internet to have a solution for all the budgets.

Predictive maintenance

Traditional maintenance fall into three categories: 1) Reactive Maintenance, you repair a broken equipment; 2) Planned Maintenance, you examine, adjust, and change elements of an equipment in a calendar basis according to the plan; and Predictive Maintenance you provide maintenance at the right moment to the right component because you can predict the future state of those equipment elements based on its behavior.

IoT solutions help to predict instead of periodically examine for adjustments, setups and wear off in a calendar basis, for that, it is required to detect failures before they happen and fix them. By continuously monitoring specific parameters of a critical equipment it is possible to analyze trends, detect patterns that might indicate a potential failure.

Continuous Base Monitoring (CBM) is a discipline that uses IoT to monitor asset conditions. IoT enables the tracking of patterns that might indicate equipment failure. Early failure prediction allows for timely action and prevents a major failure down the line. This ensures smooth running of the equipment. CBM also allows you to know when your equipment is near EOL (End of Life). This allows to plan for its replacement. The impact is observed in the reduction of maintenance cost, downtime, capital cost, and scheduled repairs. The ultimate goal is to prevent unplanned spend and downtime by tracking critical parameters in the equipment.

Predictive Maintenance follow as all the applications the IoT cycle, first you connect sensors on the machine and connects them via Internet to a Software platform. The Software aggregates data from all the sensors in the equipment and display them remotely, thresholds, are overlapped to current data to check that incoming data is within limits meaning the machine is on "healthy" condition. The data is analyzed for variations, trends and known patters either by a human or a Machine Learning algorithm to predict failure. The verdict of the analysis is transmitted to maintenance, and engineering crews responsible of the machine to let them know that all is normal or to alert them of a possible malfunctioning on a specific component. Maintenance technicians act upon the received information and provide maintenance. The loop is closed when the display shows the incoming data is normal.

According to Deloitte [57] the most important pieces of the predictive maintenance are the sensors that create the data and the communications needed to get those data to where they can be stored and analyzed.

Safety

LOTO or Lockout/tagout controls hazardous energy and protect workers from harm when machines or equipment are being prepared for service or maintenance. By connecting the asset through IoT to collect and analyze data, allows the improvement of working conditions and alert of any emergency situation. In certain equipment is necessary to wait for them to cool down or completely shut down prior to physically engage for maintenance for example. The ability of tracking temperature parameters or others in your smartphone allows you to lock the machine until is completely safe to release it for service avoiding putting maintenance crew at risk.

The use of connected wearable devices or IoT devices can monitor fatigue on workers performing a dangerous activity or closeness of the worker to a dangerous zone. Other wearables can collect information about working conditions to be analyzed over time and propose changes in schedule, air, noise, etc. By measuring biometrics with IoT devices workers can be warned about hazards, and ergonomic conditions reducing the number of accidents.

Logistics

A broad understanding of logistics as the planning, execution and control of the procurement, and stowing of material, equipment and personnel provides a perfect framework for the application of IoT. By connecting these material and resources and communicating data such location, elapsed time since harvested, or produced offers a powerful set of information to be used for different purposes:

1) Inbound material if tracked on its way to the factory allow to schedule production with minimum in transit inventories
2) Inbound material elapsed time since harvested allows to move material faster if perishable or if shelf life maybe compromise
3) Information of connected inbound material allow software platforms to store material efficiently in the warehouse to reduce pick up routes

4) Outbound products tracking allow to calculate accurate delivery times to increase customer satisfaction.
5) Warehouse as a connected asset provides temperature, humidity data per zones, connected material can then be directed to specific zones according to conditions
6) Automated storage and pick up can only be achieved by using IoT

We are certainly missing other applications, however the goal is to highlight the applicability of IoT in logistics and the importance of visibility of the material and resources in real time to take prompt decisions about where to store them, the amount of inventory in transit inbound or outbound, the tracking of shipments to have real times of the trucks transporting the finish goods parked in customs or brokers that can be used to calculate ETA (Estimated Time of Arrival), etc.

Another important contribution of IoT to logistics is the reduction of the number of transactions performed at each stage of the movement of the material from the moment a component leaves the supplier facility, along its transformation to the point when the finish good is received by the customer. The automation of the inventory transactions can be achieved now thanks to IoT and the ability to monitor all the material and assets in real time.

Transportation from logistics perspective is an accumulation of delays for delivery, from weather eventualities such hurricanes, infrastructure conditions; congested highways, closed airport, political variables, fatigued driver, etc. IoT is a powerful technology that collects location data and others of the cargo-freight-ship with the material of interest and communicates it to a central tower in the corporate headquarters where the information is aggregated with the one described above representing risk. The scenario for the material in transit is then analyzed holistically to provide a level of risk and then act if the risk is high providing alternate routes or launching redundant production at other sites or purchasing material from other vendors to mitigate the risk. Flextronics claim to have a control tower to manage its complex network of 14,000 suppliers in real time [58].

Quality Control

The cost of poor quality is hidden behind rework, adjustments, and over inspections. In order to monitor the quality behavior of our product across the production floor and beyond, the products need to talk to the different systems along this manufacturing chain. The deficit of quality has different origins, from the natural variability of the process impacting the critical parameters that define a good quality product, the lack of understanding of limits and critical features, to the use of inadequate tools for the measurement of those quality features. IoT provides the ability to capture the natural variation of a product in its habitat, i.e. production floor by connecting product-machine or product-process in real time, the data resulting of this connectivity is transmitted via Internet to (SPC) Statistical Process Control software platforms to accumulate data over time and determine if that feature is under control or not according to SPC rules. An out of control triggers an alarm that provokes an action from the owners of the process. So, in simple terms if the process isn't connected the manual entering of the data is prompt to errors and operator dependent which results sooner or later on empty charts and other lack of data.

Another emergent trend of IoT in Quality Control are the IoT Instruments. All the measurement systems in the floor or at incoming inspection are capable of connect to the Internet wirelessly. Data from all the instruments along the making of the product are collected and aggregated to form the quality behavior profile. In Medical Device Industries for example, that data is reported in the Device History Record together with other manufacturing data to prove that all the good manufacturing practices were respected. All instruments with IoT capabilities can be monitored by the OEM (Original Equipment Manufacturer) for software updates, calibration scheduling, and maintenance.

As a supplier you have to provide data or a certificate to prove that the shipment of components is within tolerances and that it complies with all the requirements imposed by the customer. By collecting data from your inspection instruments, you can transfer that data via internet to the customer who will take over it and review it to accept or reject the shipment prior to the delivery, saving time, unnecessary administrative time on disputes and eliminating redundancies along the supply chain.

With the power of big data collected thanks to the use of the internet of things, the quality behavior of the product across its manufacturing history can be used in machine learning algorithm for inspections where subjectivity plays a role, or to detect slight changes not perceive by the daily interactions. Artificial Intelligence together with the IoT has the potential to increase the reliability of inspections and consequently improving quality levels.

IoT in other areas

IoT is a technology hard to disassociate from other technologies using real time data that rule in manufacturing. IoT for example, has a tremendous success in production data collection by giving the ability to have wireless production dashboards in tablets and other displays. There are companies with geographic split productions that benefit of having a unique board with conjoint KPIs (Key Performance Metrics). Another example is the IoT role in redefining Manufacturing Execution Systems (MES) by enabling more real-time data and greater control over the most complex aspects of manufacturing operations. IoT in facilities to monitor and control lighting, HVAC equipment, secure premises with connected cameras and automated alarms for intrusions, and so on. IoT is harnessing manufacturing, providing large amount of data, big data, and the ability of harvesting that data will give a competitive advantage on the digitalization journey. Big data will be used to feed AI agents used to automate inspection, scheduling and other boring activities or where human's performance is inferior to machine learning algorithms.

Manufacturing Execution System (MES)

The Manufacturing Execution System Association MESA definition of MES [64]:

> "Manufacturing Execution Systems (MES) deliver information that enables the optimization of production activities from order launch to finished goods. Using current and accurate data, MES guides, initiates, responds to, and reports on plant activities as they occur. The resulting rapid response to changing conditions, coupled with a focus on reducing non value-added activities, drives effective plant operations and processes. MES improves the return on operational assets as well as on-time delivery, inventory turns, gross margin, and cash flow performance. MES provides mission-critical information about production activities across the enterprise and supply chain via bi-directional communications."

MES fills the gap between the systems used to plan manufacturing, and the systems used to execute the manufacturing plan. It integrates all the activities that are not in the planning layer or in the control layer so it might be seen as an intermediate step between, the ERP (Enterprise Resource Planning), and a process control system.

Control layer systems are PLCs, sensors, HMI with limited historical storage and information transfer speeds in the millisecond range while ERP systems process financial, and inventory information. They are updated in a day, week, month, or quarter basis.

Both the speed of the control systems and the planning and tracking ability of an ERP system is needed in the middle ground. This middle ground is commonly referred to as MES. The International Society of Automation on the standard ISA-95 places MES at the level 3 together with Warehouse Management (WMS) and Laboratory Information Management Systems (LIMS), as shown in the figure:

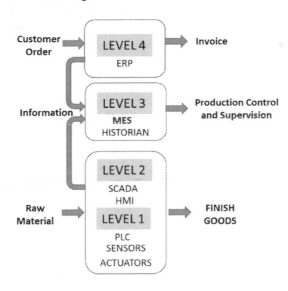

Figure 21 ISA-95 Levels

The process itself is considered the level 0 while the level 1 is the **level of automation** where all the interaction between PLC (Programmable Logic Controller), sensors and actuators occurs. It is the hardware, the wiring of the raw material transformation process. Level 2 is named the **human level** due to the interaction with humans through Human Machine Interfaces (HMI) for operators monitor the plant activities, and SCADA (Supervisory Control Automated Data Acquisition) systems to manage plant activities. Typically, HMIs are linked with one or two PLCs performing specific functions of a machine, while SCADA systems manages several connected machines allowing visualize the process, and read and transmit data to several PLC. The level 3 called **production Control and Historical level**, have two distinct components. The historian database to keep all the measurements of the sensors, production, and others that the stakeholders consider important and the MES to supervise and execute the manufacturing plan. The last level is the **accounting level**, which has programs to manage inventories, billing process, accounting and logistics.

The middle ground activities related to production control are incorporated in a computerized system that is the accumulation of the methods and tools used to accomplish production, also known as MES. A production order tracking system through the different steps of the routers, a data collection system for the OEE, all the activities not embraced by the ERP and oriented to execute the production plan are considered as MES. In simple terms, MES is the software used in manufacturing to track, control and document the transformation of raw materials to finish goods. In this sense, some non-all-inclusive list of activities would be [65]:

- **Dispatching**: Giving the command to send materials or order to certain parts of the plant to begin a process or step.
- **Scheduling**. - Sequencing and timing activities for optimized plant performance based on finite capacities of the resources.
- **Resources Allocation**.- Manages resources, including machines, tools, labor skills, materials and other equipment, and other entities such as documents that mist be available for work to start at an operation.
- **Labor Management**. - Provides the status of personnel
- **Data Collection**. - Provides a link to obtain the intra-operational production and parametric data
- **Performance Analysis**. - Provides up to the minute reporting of actual manufacturing operations results along with the comparison to past history expected business results.
- **Quality Control**. - Provide real time analysis of measurements collected from manufacturing to assure proper product quality control and to identify problems requiring attention.
- **Maintenance Management**. - Tracks and directs the activities to maintain the equipment and tools to ensure their availability.
- **Materials track and trace**. - Provides visibility to where work is at all times and its disposition. Status information may include

personal working on it; component material by supplier; lot and serial number; current production conditions; and any alarms, rework, or other exception related to the product.

- **e-DHR**. - Compilation of all records pertaining to the production of a finished medical device. With the introduction of digital manufacturing, the compilation of records moved from paper to electronic format, hence, the e-DHR.

Manufacturing is constantly under a lot of pressure to produce high quality product, cost efficiently and rapidly. Since MES increases visibility into every aspect of manufacturing, provides real time feedback, and it is specifically designed to automate activities at the production floor level, the benefits from a successful implementation are:

- **Reduce production errors**. - Scheduling, Labor, scrap, downtime, and maintenance are either giving or collected in real time from and to the shop floor. Taking the human factor out of this loop reduce the number of production errors.
- **Increase Productivity**. - By tracking materials and parts MES can reconfigure schedules to maximize use of all resources without waiting for availability or shutdowns. At the same time, collecting running rates, yield, and availability of the equipment, OEE is displayed to track performance and react on time whenever a situation impacting productivity occurs.
- **Improve compliance**. - By automating the entry of data into the device history record, it prevents typo errors for dates, initials, maintenance dates, training of the operators, etc. It facilitates the storage and retrieval of DHR electronic documents for the regulatory body audits and investigations.
- **Reduce waste and scrap**. - MES allows for precisely analyzing production lines and finished products. Therefore the system can detect any inconsistencies on the shop floor, immediately halting them to limit the number of bad parts and materials wasted.
- **Reduce Inventory**. - MES makes your inventory records updated visible. At the moment, the material is consumed in the production line, an inventory transaction is automatically executed to deplete those materials out of the inventory on hand.

There are certainly more benefits than the ones above such as eliminating the paper records from the production site, agility on the scheduling, dispatching and execution of production orders, mobility of the production data that can be displayed on different platforms for decisions takers to react on real time data, tracing of materials that in case of a shift in quality can be traced back to the supplier level or harvesting of collected data for continuous improvement.

There is no doubt that manufacturing is going to get more complex because of the trends and changes explained in previous chapters, so to continue to rely solely in the human abilities to run production flawlessly day after day is a risk that can be appease by the use of MES.

E-DHR example

One of the most important activities from the compliance point of view is the creation of the history record of each product in a medical device discrete manufacturing. In order to create such record a lot of information from different sources is collected. In the pre MES era, all these data were attached to the paper forms by the operator at each station. This situation is prone to errors of all sorts, consumes production time and is adds indirect cost. The way to collect data with MES requires the operator to scan his badge or use biometrics controls to testify his identity then the system connects with the training database that confirms that he is trained in the current revision running at that moment. The operator scans the instruments he will use to assembly the components at his station and check for calibration status of all the equipment by scanning the labels. The calibration and maintenance data from the reading of the labels is compared against databased keeping the records for all the equipment of the site. All the necessary data is collected by automated transactions. In the case that the operation require to collect data out of a testing or inspection control process, these data are pulled directly from the ATE (Automated Testing Equipment) and attached to the device history report. The advantages of such MES applications go beyond the increase of productivity or reduction of human errors. It provides a way to go back in time to check on specific manufacturing dates if required for investigations since all data is stored electronically. Even more, because the operator is checking at each step of the process, he automatically provides information on the time spend at each station or in other words he provides the cycle time that can be analyzed for continuous improvement purposes. Other applications for tracking material consumed on each product, or tracking the product across the transformation process are common in the industry.

MES Conclusions

The market offers for MES solutions are varied and it is necessary to have a clear understanding of the problem you need to solve in your manufacturing floor even before having a review with any MES supplier. It is also recommended for the manufacturing leadership to develop a roadmap and create a portfolio of the different MES modules or to be implemented based on the pain points and following the structure developed in the previous chapter. For example, if a plant or facility is generating recurrent CAPAs (Corrective Action Preventive Action) due to typo errors in the Device History Records, it has continuous investigations and audits, starting with an e-DHR module implementation provides the benefits of reducing the opportunities for error, facilitate the retrieval of documents for investigations, and improve traceability. If for example, you are experiencing inventory accuracy issues because the production associates forget to transact the consumed materials then a material inventory management system that support production floor activities is better suited as MES module solution. A lesson learned from the review of most of the market available solution is that there is no single magical MES solution that will work perfect for all your problems. Some brands are recognized for having great ways to track your materials and products in the floor while others are better suited for connecting your maintenance, training, calibration and other databases to create a consolidated report of the history of manufacturing.

Artificial Intelligence

Let's start this segment by saying that Artificial Intelligence (AI) is not an existential threat to humanity, and that dystopian scenarios are more the result of science fiction movies than the result of real applications. Rene Descartes – *I think therefore I am*, alleged that being human was the privilege of those who think. For him, existence spun around the thinking ability. The idea of losing this control is what creates stories of a dystopian society living under the governance of the machines. The potential of Artificial Intelligence is real and its effects are already here and already changing lives. Now we are able to enhance ourselves by using mental tools, tools that augments our cognitive power not only our physical abilities.

Among the trending topics in almost all business sectors, Artificial Intelligence is without a doubt in the top not only for the potential but for the level of maturity this technology is rapidly approaching. The expansion of AI has been undetectable creeping into our society lightly noticed, the adjective smart moved from being exclusive of humans to be shared with machines, and now it is common to refer to a machine as smart

Love it or hate it, AI is already part of our lives when you search on the web, or talk to your phone or using Facebook, AI is embedded in all these platforms to shorten your search time, understand better the pitch and tone of your voice or to recognize the people in the picture you are posting. We can argue these applications are in the pure digital realm, riskless, that we can stop using them and nothing wrong other than losing time will happen. you'll enter the people in your posting manually or give more input information to google to tune up your search, etc. but what about the autopilot of an airplane keeping you safer or the ABS (Automated Braking System) in your car, without them the number of people at risk is exponentially higher. AI isn't only a ludic tool that provide with comfort but an essential tool that reduce our risk in life and make it more productive. AI increases efficiency when narrows the options of a decision using millions of data or when integrates contextual information into robots to allow them to react to changes in the environment, or provides learning capabilities to inspection systems for them to recognize variations of a defect that a traditional pattern recognition system wouldn't' catch.

The adjective intelligent is applied to those being quick to comprehend and responds when in uncertain environments, or those capable of solving problems, or those having the capability of reasoning and to understand. As probably already noticed, there are multiple definitions of what it means to be intelligent. What we are looking on this chapter is to describe the uses of AI in manufacturing to indirectly define what makes manufacturing smart, what are the applications developed, how can be exploited to improve Safety, Quality, Delivery or Cost. How this tools are integrated to increase the intellectual quotient of manufacturing. What other are elements can be added.

Kevin Kelly point of view in the inevitable book [17] is that a process of cognification is transforming our entire daily life the same way mechanization changed the way we saw the conversion of the world from completely manual into a machine driven one, and then how it changed again by the additional transformation of the electrification giving us electromechanical, electronic and digital devices that made our life easier to the point that we don't conceive the world without them, robots, TVs, cars, etc. The next stage on the evolution is the cognification thanks to the harnessing of the power of data, evolution of the algorithms and processing capabilities brought by the digitalization of our products and by extension of our processes. In other words the next episode in the AI saga is how to increase the power of thinking of physical objects such machines that accompany humans and abstract entities such manufacturing that also produce, collect and use tons of data. In a simplistic approach artificial intelligence in manufacturing is the integration of cognitive power into production assets, either by extracting and processing data out of it or by increasing its data generation and processing through the insertion of sensing and processing capabilities.

In the book what to do when machines do everything [53], the authors explain the trepidation of being displaced by machines and how the luddites in England destroyed the looms because of the fear of losing their jobs by the machines. In order to transfer AI tools, concepts and experience into manufacturing, a delta in productivity is necessary, or a safer manufacturing environment or a higher level of product quality. Under all circumstances, inserting AI tools in the production floor without a clear understanding of their impact will only create a bad reputation and slower adoption by the organization, so it is important to clarify how the company will unlock the value by tapping into this technologies that sooner or later will enter our production systems.

There are different ways to outline the applicability of AI into manufacturing, however the easiest way to grasp it is to review the functional areas and check the impact and benefits of its utilization at the shop floor level to optimize manufacturing operations in production, maintenance and quality.

Production. - AI will use historical data, data from the batch of material, and equipment status data to optimize the run of that specific batch. The goal is to obtain the best product possible from run one instead of making an initial run, analyze the product and determine the necessary adjustments to optimize the output of the process. Continuous optimization of production assets is using the avalanche of data provided by increasing sensing capabilities embedded into the equipment. The capability of reconfiguring the parameters of the transformation system either an equipment or an entire process reduces lead time, reduces cost by increasing material utilization, and provides flexibility.

Even though automation concept applies beyond production, the impact of AI in production automation is palpable in the challenge of making the material available for the assembly or inspection. The supply of the material to the current automated system requires to be either fed by a human for semi-automated or picked by robotic arms or aligned and delivered by a vibrator bowl system. AI use image recognition to support robotic arms on the picking and place of material regardless of the orientation and location of the parts.

Another use of AI in production are the Autonomous Mobile robots to carry parts, detect obstacles and adjust routes. Having a fleet of robots floating around transporting material is great, however when the fleet coordinate between them to provide service by the closest robot, or the most adequate according to the payload or to improve the efficiency of the routes, we can refer to them as an intelligent fleet of AMRs.

Quality. – Measuring qualitative attributes is a nightmare for manufacturing since it relies in human abilities and perceptions to segregate defects. A defect isn't always crisp or black and white condition some products have light scratches, minor color errors other flaws unperceptive for a naked eye that forces the implementation of identical human inspection stations aiming to increase reliability. AI helps to eliminate human error by introducing pattern recognition algorithms with learning capabilities that identifies slight deviations on quality conditions unperceptive for humans. AI continuously analyze and learn from data generated by the system. This stream of data coming from the production line representing the quality of the product is submitted to the judgment of a trained algorithm that already learned from all the previous data and was fed by humans on what a defect is and how it looks like. Human inspection is slow, full of unnecessary controls, training and additional costs that makes it ineffective. According to IBM, intelligent visual inspection tools like the one they propose can reduce inspection times for manufactures by up to 80%.

Machine learning, is among the AI disciplines the one that is being deploying more applications than any other. The capability of teaching a neural network to inspect something that a human has been doing for years is a power that opens the door to let boring activities such visual inspection to machines to do it over and over every time better by learning in the transition. When a human inspect a cosmetic defect there are physical limitations and fatigue that can't warranty the inspection is performed as scripted. AI agents go beyond human vision and can work for hours and hours uninterrupted.

AI systems predict quality issues by analyzing and learning from quality and process data. It takes long time to train an inspector to interpret the results of a complicated testing, regularly the results are shared with SMEs (Subject Matter Experts) to double check on the decision to take a batch of a continuous process that can cost thousands of dollars. AI uses historical data of decisions taken by the experts, to feed the algorithms to support the decision process saving money and improving the quality of the processed batch even though it changes at every run.

Data compiled from in line inspections are used for SPC (Statistical Process Control), however these type of tools failed to process big data and retrieve trends out of it. AI mines these data and provides long term trends and recommendations using big data AI techniques.

Other simple ideas of low investment is the use of AI agents as those in Siri or Alexa to record directly information from the production floor related to the quality of the product, and store it in a way that can be accessed later when a similar defect or situation occurs in a sort of production memory. The concept is similar the way we use this technology at home but at work with speech recognition and machine learning algorithms.

Maintenance. - Reduce machine breakdowns to maximize asset efficiency is paramount for manufacturing. AI analyze data from sensors, material, and historic to determine life expectancy of critical components to prevent shutdowns. AI algorithms can automate and prioritize routine decision-making processes so your maintenance team can decide what to fix first with confidence during troubleshooting process.

Predictive maintenance is in all the operational staff conversation when high-capital assets are at stake, and when there are high cost of maintenance, or potential catastrophic impacts such production lines shutdowns, or safety implications. Many companies already made the first step of providing these assets with sensing capabilities, and data connectivity to monitor status. Data monitoring is a good first step, the transfer of data out of the equipment from those sensors to feed machine learning algorithms and take action (interact) or provide recommendations before the event occurs is better. Based on this predictability, you can schedule your maintenance in advance, and change wore components and others before a failure even happens. Intelligent algorithms processing data coming out of the important asset predict the events triggering notifications to the maintenance crew and can go as far as to order the replacement part automatically. So, in order to build up your predictive maintenance system:

• Sensors	• Connectivity	• Engine	• Visualization
Ask the experts what are the sensors required for functioning Determine the sensors that will add value	Determine if you require real time data or data historians are OK	Predictive Maintenance Algorithm to detect anomalies based on Neural Networks or others	Develop a set of tools to interact with the engine, Signal analysis, data mining, trending, predicting, visualize

Warehouse. – When dealing with managing material storage size really matters. Large warehouses use a considerable number of resources to receive, plan the storing location, place those materials into the locations, and to retrieve them when required for production purposes or distribution. AI could take the information provided by the incoming material in terms of quantity to calculate dimensions, hazard condition, perishability, and other elements together with current space availability, summon the autonomous mobile robot for the pickup of the material close to the docks the robot handshake the rack or pallet of material before pickup and transfer it to the warehouse location assigned by the AI software. The gains in efficiencies are clear in this scenario however the power beyond the faster transfer from docks to warehouse locations is the planning maximizing the use of those locations, and the faster retrieval from there based on the frequency of use of the material. The location of the products with higher rotation not only increase the efficiency by reducing the distance but reduce the congestion of robots or humans moving back and forth between those locations and production or shipping points.

When an order to create a kit for production, or a Kanban card to replenish a bin arrives to the warehouse, a machine-learning algorithm sort it in the best order to be picked. In this way, if either a robot or a person completes the action it does it in the most productive way. The route is optimized for the entire picking list reducing the amount of energy and picking time.

There are other uses of AI in Manufacturing such smart production planning to maximize asset utilization using scheduled maintenance, open production orders as well as OEE (Overall Equipment Effectiveness) to make decisions faster and with confidence in regards to where the orders have to be processed. There are plenty of AI applications in intelligent robotics as well for assembly and for moving material inside the four walls of a factory and not only for robots but algorithms inserted in other machines that convert these machines into "intelligent" assets. The number of equipment considered "smart" is increasing and communication between them as well. This interoperability will create a network of production assets that will take a set of components and raw material to transform it into a customized finish good in the most efficient way in regard to energy, time and material use without the intermediate decisions made by humans who are slow to learn and make too many mistakes. It is expected that AI will make mistakes earlier and more often to achieve optimal state faster and orchestrate the production floor efficiently.

There are innumerable AI exploitation in manufacturing the table below summarize the potential applications across manufacturing [54]:

Functional Area	Application
Warehouse	• AI systems dynamically optimize warehouse utilization, taking into account material outflows, inflows, inventory levels and turn rates.
Production	• Machines self-optimize their parameters on the basis of material input and process parameters • Robots use image recognition to automatically adapt to changing location and orientation of parts. • Autonomous Mobile robots with AI capabilities carry parts, detect obstacles and adjust routes
Maintenance	• AI systems predict maintenance needs by identifying failure patterns • Assistance system suggest solutions to incidents based on earlier failure reports.
Quality	• AI systems predict quality issues by analyzing and learning from quality and process data • AI systems detect quality defects through image recognition

Table 2 AI applications in Manufacturing

Digital Twins

Digital Twin is a virtual representation that matches the physical attributes of a "real world" factory, plant, product or component in real time, through the use of sensors, and other data collection techniques. In other words, Digital Twin is a live model that exist thanks to IoT. Twins are representations of specific assets within a facility, an entire facility, or individual product or component in the field.

The reason why replicate a manufacturing asset is important because the digital representation provides insightful information of the machine, equipment, instrument or process that otherwise it would be difficult to visualize and interact with it without altering its conditions. A digital twin can head off problems before they even occur giving the opportunity to the operation to prevent a shutdown of a line. A digital twin of an entire factory facilitates its mobility. A digital twin of a product provide dynamic information across its entire life cycle

A digital twin follows the typical IoT application cycle. Components of the asset or product use sensors to collect data about its status, location, and others. The sensors are connected to a software platform that receives and processes all the data the sensors monitor. Since the information is collected in real time, a virtual representation of the asset or product can be created and its conduct can be monitored with the contextual data received.

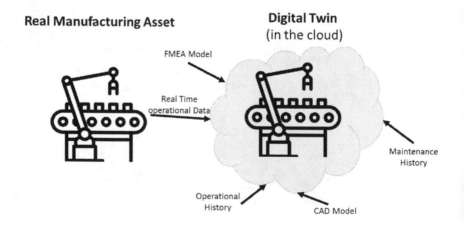

Figure 22 Digital Twin of a Manufacturing Asset

Some of the benefits of a digital twin in manufacturing are:

- Real time process simulation. The way manufacturing processes are simulated for optimization purposes is by entering all the elements and variables of the process manually then running different scenarios. With a digital twin of the process, real time simulations and what if scenarios are visualized. These simulations allow early discovery of performance deficiencies before processes are developed or while in production.
- An effective assessment of the status of a critical asset is achieved by observing and dialoguing with its twin. The evolution of its capabilities along its working life are monitored providing dynamic information on its status.
- A digital copy of a process, asset or product allows ideas to be tested before the actual manufacture began.
- Digital representations of products and assets are used for augmented reality applications.

Augmented Reality (AR)

Augmented Reality (AR) is growing with an increasing number of applications in manufacturing, and exponential adoption by the largest manufacturers in USA. Industry 4.0 provides the perfect framework to continue AR's journey towards a mature technology across the supply chain.

The goal of this segment is to provide guides for those starting the journey. Here you'll learn the difference between AR and VR, the necessary elements to build an AR application, what are the market options and some of the implementation ideas in other business segments.

The first section places AR as one of the main concepts of Industry 4.0 and explain the reasons why we can use this technology today, what are the elements that converged to make it possible.

AR has applications across different markets and across the supply chain, from working with the suppliers up to collaborating with customers. There is few industries that won't be impacted by AR, from fashion and music to education and marketing, all segments are rapidly finding innovative uses for AR.

The goal and main interest of this report is to present a picture of the applicability of AR in manufacturing, Quality and other functions. Examples, and notes on how Lean Manufacturing concepts are closely related are presented in this section

At the end, as any other digital tool, there are pros and cons of using an emergent technology, last section provides some recommendations, thoughts and conclusions.

AR within Manufacturing 4.0

AR wouldn't exist without the tremendous progress in the digitalization of manufacturing. Manufacturing 4.0 provided a suitable framework for AR by placing it a side of other cyber-physical systems such Internet of Things, digital twins, etc. Digitization of the Manufacturing environment creates the infrastructure for digital tools such AR to be successfully deployed. There's no AR without Internet, or internal network connectivity, or external communication capabilities.

With the advent of manufacturing digitalization, a wealth of digital data is available from the production systems and supporting functions. We have now, a constant flow of data from the assembly lines, testing and quality inspections that we can use it to analyze the behavior of our products across its life in production. We have electronic procedures deliver to the line in paper because there is no an electronic mean to display them, and so on. All this information remains trapped on two dimensional pages and screens limiting our ability to take full advantage of it.

A remarkable concept from the set of technologies of manufacturing 4.0 is digital twins, which refers to a digital replica of physical assets, and processes [4]. The goal of a digital twin is to create a living digital simulation model that update and change as their physical counterpart change. The power of combining AR and digital twin provides a living digital asset overlapped in front of the real physical asset, giving the user through AR the ability to interact with the asset, manipulate it for simulation purposes or setting up the asset for a change model or looking at it internally (digitally) to optimize the operation and maintenance. A digital asset is possible because of Internet of Things, another concept from manufacturing 4.0 where physical objects can live and interact with other machines and people.

Manufacturing 4.0 as well as AR have benefited of the dropping in cost of critical technologies necessary for its success: Sensors, Cost of Processing, Cost of Bandwidth, cost of storage [2]. See figure 1.

0.5X drop in cost of Sensors

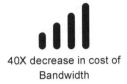

40X decrease in cost of
Bandwidth

60X Decrease in cost of
Processing

50X Decrease in cost of
Storage

**Figure 23 Eroding Cost of Key technologies leading
to the cost reduction of AR applications.**

AR versus Virtual Reality (VR)

AR and VR have two things in common: 1) Both technologies are under a tremendous growth, 2) Both alter our perception of the world. However, there is still common confusions between them, and significant differences that require a clear understanding.

VR is artificial from the point of view that 100% of the environment which the user interacts with is computer generated. In other words, VR is a full immersion in a digital setting taking over the sensing. VR takes you somewhere else, it puts our presence elsewhere through closed visors and a digital environment. Once you put the headset you are immerse and blind from the current world, i.e. the real world.

AR takes our physical world and adds "something" to it in order to enhance it, and guide action. It overlaps digital "useful" information, or in other words it augments our perception of interaction of the real world through 3D objects that appear to coexist in the same space. AR is developed into apps and used on mobile devices to blend digital components into the real world in such a way that they enhance one another, but can also be told apart easily. The overlaid information can be constructive (additive to the natural environment) or destructive (i.e. masking of the natural environment) [3].

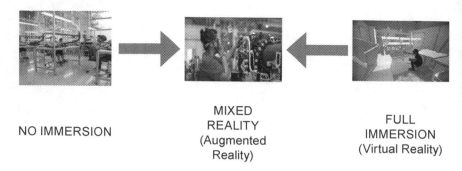

| NO IMMERSION | MIXED REALITY (Augmented Reality) | FULL IMMERSION (Virtual Reality) |

Figure 24. The Reality Spectrum

Gartner place AR and VR at the same spot as trends, critical differences exist between them achieve in manufacturing:

- VR applicability relates mostly in simulation and product design.
- AR has a larger range of applicability across the supply chain, from suppler connectivity for remote quality audits up to field service to improve customer satisfaction.

How AR works

The way we can experience AR requires three elements: 1) Reality represented by a product, process or equipment, 2) Display that it can be a helmet, glasses or tablet, and 3) Digital information that can be stored as a digital twin somewhere in a local server or the cloud.

- It starts by identifying the physical object either with a marker (RFID scanning, GPS –location) or pattern recognition
- Once the app is "connected with the object then it connects with its correspondent digital information
- If we have an inert object, meaning isn't wired or connected to transfer data then no data is streamed from it, but if we have an "alive" object then the current situation of the object is transferred to the digital reservoir
- The app retrieves the digital information from the digital reservoir and overlaps it on top of the object. It can be information related to troubleshooting, features, a work instruction on how to operate it, etc.

- The user interact with the application on the display
- The result of the interaction is sent back to the reservoir to update the digital state and if the object is not inert then it receives control information to change its state in the real world.

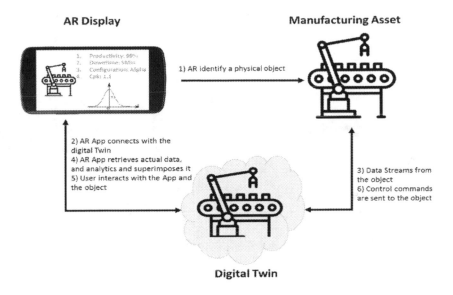

Figure 25 How AR works

A powerful and simple example of how AR works is collaboration, see figure 4, where a SME connects with production to solve quality or new product launches issues. On this case AR is being experienced by the production personnel wearing the glasses while observing the defect in the product. The torrent of data is then streamed into a monitor somewhere in the world where an SME can provide feedback in a rich multimedia environment.

Connecting...

Expert
somewhere
in the world

Technician in front
of the production
asset

Figure 26. Collaboration example

There are different ways to make an AR application. You can use a SDK (Software Development Kit) and build your own application from scratch, however you may need an IT specialist to support you to achieve your goal. You can also purchase a license for a platform that provides you with functions and features adequate for your application. If you are in the marketing business you may want to have a platform that allows you transform the way users see and use your brand. If you are in the manufacturing business you may be looking to overlap digital information in the form of instructions, or guidelines for your production crew or technicians, if you are in the field service you want to communicate, and interact with the field technical and the product under scrutiny to understand the problem.

On other side of the AR application you can use a display as simple as you telephone or you can have hands free solutions like the hololenses from Microsoft or different glasses integrated with communication capabilities as well as displaying capabilities. Our recommendation if you are starting your journey is to invest low, test your solution with couple thousand dollars of investment and then move up into more powerful solutions.

In summary, you need two entities: a platform and a display as shown in figure below.

Software Platform **+** **Display** **=** **AR Solution**

Figure 27 Displays and Platforms

AR Market

AR is making its way in the market place by working with top brands and companies. The global AR market is estimated to witness growth at a CAGR of 85.4% over the period of 2016 to 2022 according to the BIS Research report "Global Augmented reality and mixed reality market-Analysis and Forecast (2018-2025). Zion Market Research report valued AR market around USD 3.33B in 2015 with expectations of USD 133.78B by 2021. Other more conservative analysis forecast AR market to reach $60.55 billion by 2023 at a CAGR of 40.29%.

The business models under which companies are making money out of AR follow the Software industry model with value propositions (bundle of services and products) based on licensing. There are those who offer the ready to use solutions and those who sell an SDK (Software development Kit) that you use to create your customize solution. The customers are from a broad spectrum of industries and the distribution channels are through the internet.

Multiple vendors are available from applications in your mobile where you can overlay cartoon faces to your real face and merge them, applications to convert static toys into digital dynamic objects, solutions to highlight features of a product either cars or others, offers to bring to life printed objects when you read a magazine or flyer, and so on. Our focus on this report is to give you alternatives for manufacturing, here some companies working on this arena:

Company	Description	Mfg. Area	Web link
Ubimax	It offers 4 different solutions for warehousing, assembly, Quality inspection and Remote assistance	Assembly, Quality, warehousing, Maintenance	http://www.ubimax.com/en/
Scope AR	Its solution allows companies to create their own AR-based smart instructions for a variety of tasks from installation to maintenance. The platform requires no coding experience	Assembly, Quality, Maintenance	https://www.scopear.com/
OPS Solutions	It guides a worker through a task step by step and eliminate the need for printed work instructions and can also ensure workers do not miss key steps in an assembly or maintenance process. Its principle is projection of information.	Assembly	http://lightguidesys.com/
Ngrain	It uses a software that captures numerous, granular 3D data points of an object to create a detailed 3D model that can then be delivered via the software. From there users can use AR glasses, tablet, or other wearable display to examine a virtual simulation of the object in a real-time environment.	Simulation	http://www.ngrain.com/producer-pro/

AR Applications

The purpose of technology is to make our life better, AR has a widespread of applications from entertainment to manufacturing. The predicted explosive growth requires to be supported by a group of applications across different industries, here some short examples:

Entertainment	This is the world of gaming, we've got in this arena successes such as Pokemon GO, Niantic and other augmented games.

Healthcare	Most of the ideas are oriented to support the surgeon wearing AR glasses like **Viipar** that allows a surgeon in a different location to complete a surgery via augmented hands projected onto the patient. Others are into the nursing care like **Accuvein** that helps nurses to provide more accurate intravenous injection.
Retail and Marketing	The goal is to create a positive experience by the user to enforce the brand. A lot of examples of applications already exists, some of the spearheading companies are Coca Cola and Mercedes. The reality is that almost ALL companies have a strategy on this sector.
Military	The goal here is to enhance humans when confronting war activities. Soldiers receive orders via the glasses, overlapping information of territory, weapons, and others.
Education	Museums are a fabulous example to expand the knowledge of their expose using audio, or overlapping extra information related to the piece under observation. Teachers have the opportunity to do the inverse and bring the museum to the classroom by providing digital 3D versions related to the class of the day.
Fashion and Music	Check how the clothes look in you or bring your favorite band into the stage at your local bar can be an experience that you don't want to miss.
Manufacturing	The applications on this segments are oriented to impact your profitability, and customer service: training, quality, maintenance, logistics, filed service. They touch multiple areas and the solutions are available for leading companies to develop solutions. We'll see this in detail next

AR in Manufacturing

It is undisputable that AR is transforming all the processes involved in the production and distribution of a product, from suppliers to customers, AR is providing solutions to deal with complexities such high mix environment or distributed manufacturing with experts and production at different locations, and so on. The unemployment in decline as shown in the Labor of statistic chart is creating a serious threat of turnover of the workforce that impact efficiency due to the lack of training and instability.

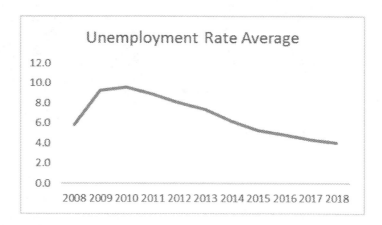

Figure 28 Unemployment rate average from 2008 to 2018

AR is aligned with the new manufacturing landscape and enters into maturity at the same time that Millennials are a larger percentage of the workforce. In Manufacturing, AR promises to provide significant boosts in operational efficiency by making information available to employees needing task support in context in real time

A headwind for AR in Manufacturing is the lack of awareness on the areas of impact, but above all the lack of understanding of the circumstances that makes this technology profitable.

Traditional massive predictable make to stock manufacturing models are eroding on behalf of less predictable, high mix, low volume make to order models. These environments are challenging because of the shorter learning curves, productivity losses as well as because of the need to react faster whenever a change occurs. AR handles this complexity by:

- Delivering assembly instructions, and drawings, directly to the production floor faster in digital way.
- Overlapping digital images of tooling instead of paper written description during maintenance procedures.
- Connecting Subject Matter Experts (SME) with technicians to solve technical or quality issues or with customers to provide guidance.
- Guiding the operator step by step in the right order to perform a line clearance or model change in an equipment.

Augmented Reality is suitable for high mix, low volume because it forces higher levels of communication between the participants of the manufacturing eco-system.

Augmented Assembly: Today the paper based procedures go through a large ordeal before released to the point of use, and sometimes it takes days before the latest revision makes it to the floor which means days of products in hold, and days of production under a manufacturing deviation, as well as hours and hours of overhead to document such deviation.

By guiding the operator step by step on the instructions of rare configurations for example, the number of errors diminish, productivity increase, the training hours got reduced, as well as the impact of turnover.

Lean Manufacturing: One concept in Lean is Built in Quality which from a simplistic point of view, its goal is to provide the operator of the guidelines to reject receiving bad subassemblies or components and prevent him/her of moving bad parts to the next operation. When dealing with complex operations, the idea of providing a set of instructions for build in quality purposes becomes difficult. AR provides a 3D visualization on how the sub-assembly should look like prior to move it to the next station. AR also provides the set of instructions with tooling visualizations.

One of the most powerful lean tools is Standardized work. By documenting the best practice standardized work creates a baseline for continuous improvement. During the Kaizen phase, the operator and wear the AR glasses allowing the Lean expert to observe the operator at his/her natural environment, the expert can see and follow whatever the assembler is doing to accomplish the task, that information is analyzed to create the best practice that will represent the flow of instructions that will also be delivered using AR.

Augmented Maintenance: How many times you have seen people looking for tooling even in the shadow boards developed after the latest Visual Management Kaizen? When building a complex product, having the image of the tool you need instead of a written description makes a huge difference, and if you add the capability of overlapping the tool on top of the right components, or launching a quick video from your location on how to use it, or labeling the components the technician is looking at, or giving him safety warning, then it can really impact process lead time. Maintenance is also all about technical knowledge, that knowledge is not always available in site when needed. AR provides technicians and engineers a tool to connect with SMEs, suppliers and Integrators to solve equipment issues faster reducing shutdown times, reducing cost by buying the right spare part instead of relying on guessing, etc.

Lean manufacturing: A popular Lean concept is SMED which goal is to reduce the amount of time to setup an equipment to work with a different product model. The essence is to convert as many change over steps as possible to be performed while the equipment is running and standardize the internal ones requiring the machine down. AR can have a huge impact as a tool to check on all the external activities sequence and instructions, and by providing 3D visualization of the components to be adjusted or change on the internal ones aligned with the product configuration. AR reduces the opportunity for error, training, and downtime.

Augmented Training: Out of the production floor, training is an important element by providing knowledge on the product functioning, product configurations, regulations, Quality Manual, and others. AR transfers the innovations in other industries to provide a more comprehensive learning process. The impact is a more knowledgeable workforce facing out of production floor task with higher levels of efficiency leading eventually into a more talented personnel.

Remote assistance: These same uncommon products are regularly forgotten meaning that since they don't run every day, the knowledge disappear with attrition. Having the production floor people connected to the product knowledge holders with audio, video and interactivity capabilities, gives AR an advantage that no other tool can provide. This assistance can happen in real time in front of the "problem" reducing the time the production line is down or the suspected inventory.

Product line changes: The underutilization of production assets due to constant reconfigurations in high mix environments is impacting productivity. The efforts to standardize and reduce these production time losses using quick Change over Lean methodologies has been relatively successful reducing the cost impact. It indeed reduced downtime by standardizing it but created extra steps and control check lists. AR can reduce time even more, and errors on these transitions by guiding the operator step by step in the right order for the right product configuration without need of consulting paper based tables or asking the supervisor or engineering team.

AR in Quality

Supplier Quality. - A good and reliable supplier is essential to maximize the value deliver by the components received. In certain industries, it becomes even more important due to the regulatory environment and the activities related to compliance. The range of activities in this area include supplier audits, incoming inspection, solve technical issues in timely manner with suppliers to eliminate non conformances, and monitor and improve Supplier KPIs.

When dealing with a complex supply network around the world, one of the main hurdles in the relationship between suppliers the components receiver that hinders collaboration is distance. AR provides an environment for both parties to dynamically interact and solve quality situation in shorter time than having a representative travelling back and forth with excessive cost and time losses.

- Multimedia rich collaboration tools provide a platform to dynamically check on specifications, eliminate ambiguity, and solve technical issues by showing defects or discrepancies in real time. The use of AR increase efficiencies by reducing the time to solve technical issues, removes the tedious travelling, and reduces inventories by solving RTVs (Return to Vendor) and discussing Corrective Actions in a more at ease environment.
- AR applications for audit purposes are innovative from the point of view that we can virtually be at the supplier site in a digital version instead of traveling and spending days in an airplane and hotel. The supplier wearing AR glasses will guide the auditor at a distance place through his/her facility to check on the evidence about corrective actions, to check on implemented safety measures, and to confirm that all non-conformances are addressed. The return on investment will come on the overhead line in the budget and the zero defect mentality within the supply base that will reduce the number of CAPAs, RTVs, and the overall impact further in the supply chain.

Quality Control. - When dealing with maintaining good quality levels from end to end of the transformation processes of a product, it is important to deliver clear and precise instructions to the point of use. The simplest control is to provide a drawing to that point of use with the desired features we want to measure or inspect.

- Inspection when performed by humans frequently contains subjective evaluations of aesthetic conditions or relies in interpretation. Most of these controls are visual inspections requiring relevant information, clear guidelines, check lists, and visualizations to support them. AR provides a great framework to deliver these type of information in real time, allowing free hand interaction, and access to remote assistance if necessary.

AR in the Warehouse

The numerous activities in a warehouse go from receiving material from the docks, document it, and storing it at the right location according to its restrictions (flammable, high value, etc.), weight and dimensions to the picking sequencing according to the production orders of the day. These operations are estimated to account for about 20% of all logistics costs, and the task of picking accounts for 55 % to 65 % of the total cost of warehousing operations according to De Koster, René et.al. (2006) [44]. There are three areas where AR could improve your logistic operation: training the new employees on where the different locations and materials are in the warehouse without the presence of a trainer. Overlaying digital modifications on top of the warehouse environment to test and adjust planned redesigns in order to reduce the cost of warehouse redesign and planning, and to optimize the picking process.

A clear inefficiency of the picking process is the worker walking with the picking list in hand around the warehouse looking for the listed components with no other support than his memory, and labels in the locations for reference. The vast majority of warehouses still use the pick-by paper approach which is slow and error prone. Furthermore, picking work is often undertaken by temporary workers who usually require cost-intensive training to ensure they pick efficiently and without making errors [45].

Picking process. - AR provides hands free digital support while reducing the number of picking errors by confirming order and material. The worker can see the picking list in the display —glasses or tablet, and navigate to a targeted location through the best route provided by the software platform. The optimization of the route for the picking of the entire list reduces the total walking distance and picking time. Once in front of the target location, the worker can check if it is the right location by barcode, vision, or other identification system provide by the display. The worker finally scan the batch of components extracted from the location to validate the transaction automatically and deplete that inventory from the warehouse in the ERP system.

AR in Product and Process Design

AR is changing the way we are looking the development of products and processes. The ability of overlaying aesthetic features in a product under development or not yet purchased equipment in a process that is under construction provides vital information for the final dimensions, shape and function of the product or process. The goal is to provide relevant feedback prior to frozen the design by providing a visualization of the product or process digitally. This capacity to run simulations on digital features reduce significantly the development iterations and number of physical prototypes. In short it reduce the development cycle time, cost and increase the quality of the product coming out of the development stage. It also provides the opportunity to show the digital prototype to multiple stakeholders to receive on time, and unrestricted feedback.

Development cycle time. When presenting a physical prototype of a product or a mock-up of a process issued of a 3P Kaizen workshop, regularly a face to face time is required to provide feedback. At the moment a digital version is available it can be transferred to the stakeholders, customers and others to received immediate feedback reducing the number of iterations and time significantly. The customer can "play" with the model in its digital form moving features in a product, equipment locations in a process, the final user can observe from different points, check for safety concerns, ergonomics opportunities and functional improvements. This capacity of giving access to relevant information of an inexistent process or product allows to remove waste.

Product Quality. When presenting a digital model on top of the prototype you can immediately realize the difference. When you have a 3D parametric model of the product with the critical to Quality features highlighted, then you can objectively communicate to the supplier about the discrepancies against the received physical product, and have a more productive conversation to converge in a higher quality product faster than without using AR. In a process, having the ability to add elements to an equipment under development like poka-yokes, or simple buttons at the operator reach will facilitate the operation and indirectly impact quality.

AR in Field Service

Probably the segment that benefits the most of the maturity of AR technology. In the field service, the time to respond and the quality of the response are the key of the success, and fortunately AR have a huge impact in both of them:

Service response time. - AR permits the customer to be guided when troubleshooting a malfunctioning product or solving a specific situation on how to use the product. The long waiting times are a matter of the past with the collaborative environments provided by AR where an expert on the other side conducts the final user through the repair, collapsing the time it takes to put a product or process back in function. The other advantage of using AR during field service is that a paper thick manual is no longer necessary and almost any technician can provide service in a shorter time with guidance provided through the glasses, tablet or other display improving MTTR (Mean Time to Repair). The technician no longer need to be a highly skilled experienced worker but an entry level with basic knowledge on the product or process increasing the crew and indirectly impacting the availability of personnel to provide the service.

Quality of the Service- Qualified field technicians alone against a complex problem have now an ally that provides an extension of their competencies. Looking at the problem with the glasses and transmitting the visuals to the headquarters where other experts reside, the probability of solving the problem increases and subsequently the quality of the service improves. By following the instructions delivered into the AR lenses, the field technicians reduce the number of errors and secures the right sequence is followed to prevent damages to the product during service.

From the field service provider point of view the decline in the number of travels to the customer's house, clinic, or facility reduces travel cost and shutdown time of critical equipment, in summary, the overall operational cost related to service. The quality and time of service impact gets reflected in customer satisfaction as well. The number of RTVs (Return to Vendor) is expected to decrease avoiding the administrative cost and negotiation time related to this activity.

Reduce Expert Travel Cost   Improve MTTR (mean Time to Repair)   Increase Customer Satisfaction   Get the job done right the first time!

Figure 29 Benefits of using AR in Field Service

AR Conclusions/Recommendations

AR is not free! Yes, you are thinking on moving into AR because you have a complex portfolio of products and you have New Product Development and Operations at different locations but be aware that:

- Your capital investment if not chosen wisely can be rapidly obsolete. There are too many choices out in the market and a lot of false promises.
- If you are going to deploy drawings, work instructions, and others directly to the production floor. You need to digitize them first, and the information needs to be reliable. There's a lot of pre-work even before thinking on applying AR. We recommend to have a paperless strategy first.
- You can't afford to have Internet shutdowns, glitches or unreliable connectivity across your facility
- At this moment there is no standard available for AR, however IEEE is developing a family of standards that will address aspects such as safety, and how different technologies should be defined. Until these standards are defined, you are basically on your own
- You need a reliable technical group "on the other side" to avoid unintelligent conversations leading to nothing. It is cool to have the ability to connect and share multimedia, however is useless when nobody knows how to solve the problem.

AR is also a technology of our times and without a doubt a tool of the factory of the future, however don't get caught on the hype, do the pre-work of having a reliable documentation and infrastructure systems, find a suitable application that you can promote before thinking on massive deployments. The impact on maintenance, production, quality, and field service is evident, and the required capital to create the infrastructure is relatively low, however a massive deployment isn't recommended until a platform and display

Automated Manufacturing -Robotization

MUCH OF THE world is witnessing a wave of technological transformation that is on the scale of the Industrial Revolution but more rapidly. The only thing that isn't coming at us faster is the ability to respond [23]. In Bloomberg June 2017 edition, Peter Coy states that work may eventually be automated, but it needs first to solve the problem of labor shortages and "skill mismatch" [24].

According to a PWC survey, about 45% of work activities can be automated, and CEOs plan to cut jobs over the next five years because of robotics. 16% of those surveyed had the opposing view that they planned to hire more people because of robotics [22]. The debate about the impact of automation and specially robotics is effervescent to the point that Bill Gates proposed in an interview with Quartz to tax robots as a way to as a way to at least temporarily slow the spread of automation and to fund other types of employment [30]

Automation as conceived at the dawn of the third industrial revolution after the entrance of the Programmable Logic Controller (PLC) was a perfect fit for mass production. However, manufacturing started to change, and now automation needs to adapt to the new requirements of low volume and significant mix of product configurations. By harnessing the power of more flexible, capable and cheaper robots, automation has been able to respond to the continuous requirement of higher levels of productivity. According to Mckinsey, the price of robots has fallen by half in real terms in the past 30 years [25]. This opens the door for a larger range of applications since new robots are easier to integrate, and allows implementations in low cost regions.

How companies respond in a time when artificial intelligence and robotics kick in and exponentially more manufacturing jobs move into automation? How they can build the internal capabilities to reduce the skills mismatch and benefit of this new wave of technology coming into maturity bringing new pools of profitability? These are some of the questions we considered while outlining this section.

Market forces and society changes are impacting the way we manufacture products by increasing complexity and demanding flexibility. In order to keep the pace on these changes Robotics has emerged as one of the tools due to the exponential changes in Sensing, Information Technologies and others that are crafting faster, more flexible, "smarter," robots creating an technological force that opens a larger field of applications beyond the assembly repetitive functions.

The current and future relationship between workers and machines challenge our basic assumption about technology: that machine are tools that increase the productivity of workers. Instead machines themselves are turning into workers, and the line between the capability of labor and capital is blurring as never before [21].

The way we think and act about manufacturing as powered by labor is changing, the old process models driven by human capital are moving into hybrid production flows with a larger and larger contribution from Robots.

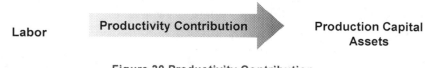

Labor   **Productivity Contribution**   **Production Capital Assets**

Figure 30 Productivity Contribution

The implications of these new models are multiple impacting the way we approach safety, the way we think about continuous improvement, the way we search for talent, training, and others.

Companies can't seat on the sidelines neglecting the benefits of these new ways of doing manufacturing with more automation and robotics instead of pure labor. The cost is too high in the mid and long term, they need to start now, and they need to rethink their manufacturing strategy.

Even though robotics is an ample topic that applies to multiple areas of a business, we restrict this report to implications related to manufacturing only. The goal of is to provide guidance, and analyze the trends and capabilities of the impact of Robotics in manufacturing. What are the current and midterm steps you need to take into order to prevent to fall into the group of laggards playing catch up?

Social and Market forces behind Robotics revolution in Manufacturing

Undoubtedly Robotics plays a role in the future of employment as well as social factors play a role in the shaping of the demand of robotics in Manufacturing. So, what are the social and market forces driving the demand of robots, and what is the relation of manufacturing with these forces?

Aging of population in industrialized countries. - The next 40 years the world will be transformed by demographic changes. According to a United Nations report in 2013, the current world population of 7.2 billion is projected to increase by one billion over the next 12 years and reach 9.6 billion by 2050. The ratio of working age people to retirees will be very different from what it is today [21]. This will require more robots to perform ergonomic challenging operations, transfer material and do dexterity required activities. According to a report from United Nations, Department of Economic and Social Affairs Population Division [26]. Between 2015 and 2030, the number of people in the world aged 60 years or over is projected to grow by 56 percent with Japan being the country with the higher percentage of elder. No wonder Japan has a clear Robot Strategy issued by Japan's Economic Revitalization [27] to deal with the situation.

Increase in customization. - Customer is no longer a passive recipient of a linear process that starts with innovation and ends with a good product. Now, he/she intervenes at the design level creating a circular innovation that translates in a large number of configurations which translates in manufacturing complexity. More product variety requires production line reconfigurations, machine shutdowns, procedures learning. The impact in productivity due to complexity is a constant pain and huge challenge. This change in manufacturing requires an easy re-deployable robot, easy to program and safer to be in the line as a solution to reduce learning curve and other productivity losses.

Increasing middle class in emergent markets. - A large number of countries are moving out of poverty and by that requesting more products aligned with their culture, language and needs. This "new" features powered by an increase in consumption in 2015 was about $35 trillion, or about $12,000 per head according the report from the Global Economy and development at Brookings [28]. In order to pass successfully these products into manufacturing, a significant increase of complexity is created. At the same time, these emergent economies have been increasing little by little the cost of labor paying extra to maintain production. This situation is making robotic business cases with better and faster returns as it is the case now for industrialized economies. The big problem on these economies isn't too much to launch robotic initiatives but the lack of talent to complete such projects.

Technology Forces behind Robotics revolution in Manufacturing

The word robotics was derived from the word robot, which was introduced by Czech writer Karel Capek in his play R.U.R (Rossum's Universal Robots), published in 1920[29]. An Industrial robot is an automatically controlled, reprogrammable, multipurpose, operator in three or more axes, which may be either fixed in place or mobile for use in industrial automation applications.

Industrial robots are moving out of the cages and going from simple pick and place applications into a more collaborative environments. They are also increasing their mobility integrating more visual recognition abilities as well as including more and more cognitive capabilities allowing them to easily integrate more complex task.

Advances in robotics are pushing the frontier of what machines are capable of doing in all facets of business and the economy. Physical robots have been around for a long time in manufacturing, but more capable, more flexible, safer, and less expensive robots are now engaging in ever expanding activities and combining both mechanization, cognitive and learning capabilities—and improving over time as they are trained by their human coworkers on the shop floor, or increasingly learn by themselves. But why now, what are the trends that support this recent upsurge?

In this section we defined at the beginning a robot as a physical programmable machine that execute task autonomously but we forgot to mention that autonomy and programmability require extensive processing, algorithm efficiency and storage capabilities that have exponentially exploded allowing the development of smarter robots with larger abilities.

Technology forces such as artificial Intelligence, Moore's Law and improvements in sensing applied to a robot have enhanced and expanded Robots applicability. Thus, if we add these forces to the manufacturing landscape we arrive to a good momentum for the rise of robots in the four walls of the factories as shown in figure below:

Technology forces · Sensing · AI · Storage · Processing

Manufacturing Landscape

Productivity Contribution — Mfg Capital Assets — Labor — Time

RISE OF ROBOTS IN MANUFACTURING

Figure 31 Technology Forces and Manufacturing Landscape supporting Robots rise

Besides the logical utilization of industrial robots as human labor substitution, many manufacturing operations are experiencing scarcity of good return opportunities after years of a Process Excellence Culture based on Toyota principles or Lean. It is evident that we need to start thinking out of the traditional robotic applications and move into collaborative environments, hybrid production systems, more flexible that integrates robots and humans in a highly productive environment.

Robots are changing the way manufacturing conceives the concept of value added. The question now is not how do we preserve a value added operation but how do we make it even more valuable by doing it faster, easier, and better through the use of robots. Productivity is no longer a labor exclusivity, and the manufacturing models are moving from heavily flexible human oriented models into highly flexible hybrid more efficient models as seen in the figure below. Robots used to be hard to program with lines and lines of code, having a flexible changing the product, sometimes meant days of shutdown, days that now because of the change in demand we can't afford.

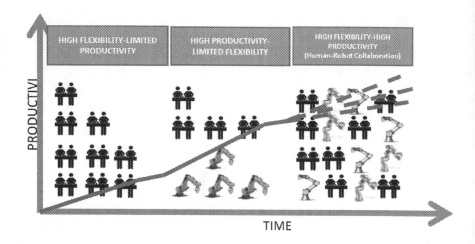

Figure 32 Productivity Hybrid Model

Robotics strategy

With consulting groups and leaders analyzing the impact of technology and robotics in various industries, and with a third more expected sales-growth in robots from 2016 to 2019 (compared to the last 17 years according to International Federation of Robotics) it is imperative for businesses to develop a robotics Strategy in order to build their internal capabilities and reduce skills mismatch. Businesses positioned correctly will benefit from this new wave of smart robotics bringing new pools of profitability.

Even though the advancement of new robotics technologies has caused the robots to be widespread, it is necessary to orderly deploy and rationalize the utilization of robotics. It is crucial to increase awareness in your workforce and leaders and potentiate your talent. Equally important is to create policies and guidelines that will standardize applications, technologies and supplier requirements.

An organized placement of robots at the right applications aligned with your company's strategy will allow you to potentiate and take full advantage of Robotics. At the same time the ability to execute such Robotic strategy in conjunction with the increase in manufacturing complexity, and the use of other technologies emerging from Industry 4.0 will allow your company to improve profitability and face competitiveness.

Therefore, we propose a strategy that works in four distinct phases going from assessment to the institutionalization of Robotics as core competency of your organization. We are confident that by executing this strategy, you I pave the success towards long term performance delivery.

Transform
Assess, baseline and revamp the processes driving your Operations

Standardize
Make Robotics the New Standard; Create Guidelines; Develop Policies

Enable
Infuse your workforce, enable your talent, and educate your leaders

Scale
Leverage the Benefits, Institutionalize Robotics

Figure 33 Robotics Strategy

Transform. The phase of transformation intends to answer the question of what areas within your operations should be tackled first in alignment with business strategy. This phase outlines the steps, and best practices, to ensure a harmonious and accelerated deployment. This phase also attempts to select the type of robotics technology that can best be used for the manufacturing task being considered [31].

- **High labor content** (Straightforward application where robots may be used to supplement human workers): Technologies such as traditional SCARA and Cartesian solutions, or Collaborative Robots, may be selected depending on factors such as cycle time, level of collaboration, risk analysis, redeployment needs, and investment.
- **Human skills gaps** (Operations where humans are limited due to component size, weight, or dexterity constraints): Exoskeletons for heavy components management, and high speed robotic arms for extremely fast operations are carefully chosen.

- **Hazardous Operations** (Operations that place a priority on safety): The applicability of robots in this environments requires a deeper understanding of the technology and process. This category includes ergonomic opportunities to reduce injury or operations which handle hazardous material. Traditional Industrial Robots can play a role here, as well as tele-robotics to remotely handle dangerous materials.
- **Critical Operations** (Operations requiring exceptional precision, speed or flexibility): Placing chips with an accuracy of a tenth of a millimeter would be considered a critical operation. Light robots with low inertia and special grippers are adequate.

At the end of this phase, you should have audited, and categorized, the previous installed robotic implementations and technologies, identified all the potential opportunities in your organization, and determine what technologies are the most adequate for those proposed projects. You should also start the deployment of a small number of implementations based on prioritization.

Enable: To make the most of the upcoming revolution in robotics, organizations need robot-savvy workers at all levels. From the production floor to the C-Suite, a change in mindset is required to ensure a successful cultural transition toward robotic acceptance. Developing a process to retain, attract, train, and recognize talent will be necessary. Develop Robotics training and link it to career development. It is also important to identify, and establish, collaboration with Universities, providers, and research centers.

A process that strengthen talent, accelerates training in robotics, generates collaboration to close the gap in the technological landscape, and recognizes employee value, needs the following focus areas:

- **Training**. - It is not a secret that automation may reduce the labor force. Companies need to train today to be prepared for tomorrow. The use of well proven platforms to spread technical knowledge and link training to performance is a successful initiative demonstrated at companies such as ATT with its nano-degree program.
- **Recruitment**. - The skills necessary to adopt robotics go beyond STEM (Science, Technology, Engineering, and Math) – there is also a need for employees with critical and analytical thinking.

Although these people are already scarce, recruitment competition will become fiercer in the future. There must be a strategy to internally develop these resources, as well as a process to externally recruit from local and top universities.

- **Recognition.** - Workers have motivation beyond monetary remuneration. Emotional factors like engagement, quality of life, and status are equally if not more important to many workers. Be sure to link recognition to robotic implementations and ideas.
- **Best Practices.** - Betting success on individual abilities is a risky business. Training or recruiting a small workforce isn't enough if process and procedures are not put in place. Knowledge sharing and networking will also facilitate Robotics implementations.
- **Collaboration.**–Working with Universities and suppliers to co-develop solutions early in the process will help reduce your biggest challenges.

At the end of this phase, you should have a roadmap detailing your human resources development plan as it is applied to robotics strategy. This should include a training program, as well as a list of potential collaborations with providers and universities.

Standardize: At the same time our manufacturing environment changes, our policies need to adapt to provide new mechanisms to improve organizational operation. For example, organizations must develop inclusive validation procedures to take into account autonomous robots, develop safety policies for Collaborative Robots, develop guidelines to expedite analysis of robotic applications, and develop robot risk analyses aligned with International Standards. These are some examples of standardization:

- **EHS Policies and Procedures.** - Robotics solutions are now interacting more actively with humans; they now operate in the middle of the production line collaboratively. They are no longer static production assets, they now move around the production floor and warehouses. In order to take into account these "smart" technologies, and be ready to accelerate implementation, changes to safety and ergonomic procedures are required. Environment, Health and safety (EHS) will need to better understand the minimum considerations for applicability of these technologies.
- **Quality, Policies, and Procedures.** - New Robotic solutions are re-deployable and can be at different lines in different production

shifts. Installation qualification procedures will need to be updated to allow for this possibility.

- *Robotic Guidelines.* – Here are some additional guidelines to help in your journey:
- *Application Assessment.* – This provides an assessment on cycle time, payload, precision, accuracy, trajectory complexity, reach, cleanroom environment, etc.
- *Robotics ROI guideline.* –It provides a clear idea of all the expenses you are going to incur (arm, gripper, fixtures, monitoring systems, safety ancillaries, other peripherals, etc.); operational expenses, (maintenance, licenses, others), and automatically calculates the return of the investment.
- *User Requirement Specification.* - Not all robotics opportunities are equal. This helps to clarify important information to eliminate ambiguity and provide priority guidance.
- *Design for Automation.* - It provides tips, and best practices on how to design components to enable automation.

At the end of this phase, you should have the essential standards required to develop policies, procedures, and guidelines to deal with risk, quality, implementation, and return of investment.

Scale: There is no valuable strategy without implementation. In order to have a significant impact at the right scale, a team needs to promote collaboration, good practices and incentivize implementation across the organization. The best way is to have a committed group of individuals accountable for deployment. This group needs to:

- Prove the value of robotics in order to win support and gain buy-in through quick wins that can deliver early benefits, which in turn can fund a broader program.
- Create a COE as a means to scale up robotic implementations and promote policies in alignment with the vision of the organization, and its Strategic imperatives.
- Develop the Robotic Technology roadmap for the next five to ten years.

At the end of the fourth phase, a Center of Excellence or accountable group is created that delivers the first implementations and generates a roadmap according to the needs of the organization.

Collaborative Robots

Robots are becoming present in our everyday life: they are used for domestic tasks, for support activities, and now to collaborate with humans at work. According to Boston Consulting Group, BCG[16] the total cost of manufacturing labor in 2025 could be 16% lower, on average as a direct result of installation of robots in highly automatable tasks in high wages countries.

Noticing the growing integration of robots in hybrid manufacturing models and the bulky solutions provided by Industrial Robot options. Robotics companies started to provide solutions to interact or collaborate to create a collaborative environment between humans and robots in the same space.

Collaborative Robots or Cobots are expected to grow in the next few years due to its affordability and easy to use. They are easy to relocate or deploy with a small footprint and with safety features beyond traditional industrial robots such as torque sensing, collision detection among others. The fast setup is based on the easiness to teach new task because they are simple and can be programmed by no experts.

In contrast, industrial robots are bigger surrounded by a cage to protect humans. As commented by Kevin Kelly in his New York Time seller the Inevitable, robots are simply too dangerous to be around, because they are oblivious to others [17]

Manufacturing simplification means the conscious seeking of the simplest, easiest, and quickest method of adding value to the transformation process of a product. It is accomplishing more tasks with less effort in a given amount of time. It is our claim that Cobots provide different ways to simplify manufacturing:

- **Simplification of Setup**. —More product variants translate into new manufacturing tasks or deviations, in other words, complexity rises. A Cobot can easily be repurposed for new tasks or slight changes making the process down time shorter or meaningless and productivity higher. When this same Cobot can be hand guided for a new operation by an associate of production it saves set up time but it also intensifies employee empowerment.

- **Simplification of deployment**. – Deployment refers to bring or place resources into action in a position. In manufacturing terms, it means to place people, equipment and tooling at the right location expeditiously. Whenever a production asset or equipment is relocated, a huge effort is required. Relocation maybe necessary because of capacity constraints, special utilities location or heavy assets such as presses or others that force us to work at different points of the production floor. Cobots easily overcome this lack of mobility due to their low weight (between 10-20 Kgs), and because they can be mounted in different ways to a table, ceiling or floor. Most of the Cobots only require AC power and have a small footprint. This flexibility or easiness of deployment allows a Cobot to work in a production line in first shift and work in a different one in the second shift for example.
- **Simplification of Training**. - The loss of productivity attributable to learning curves when a company has high turnover, constant engineering changes for immature products, quality deviations or excessive number of product configurations is a challenge for manufacturing in general. When you "hire" a Cobot, you eliminate turnover concerns. Anyone can train a Cobot, most of them only require to be hand guided to an approximate trajectory and location. They learn the motions and sequence and repeat it, and improve it! Engineers coding thousands of lines to secure repeatability, and accuracy are a thing of the past, now you don't need to be a robotics literate to redeploy and teach a Cobot a new task. These tasks since taught to the Cobot by its coworkers are better assimilated by the rest of the human crew because they know what its cyber collaborator is doing, and how affects them.
- **Simplification on safety**. – In manufacturing terms, simplify safety means obtaining higher safety levels with less effort or less complexity, with no compromises; the goal continues to be zero accidents and no ergonomic issues. When you deal with cobots, safety is priority number one as well. In contrast to a regular equipment or industrial robot, Cobots have integrated features that can feel abnormal forces in its path. In fact, they are programmed to stop when they read an overload in terms of force. A cobot detects collisions, springs back when a contact occurs and has negligible pinch points. The cobots are also designed to dissipate forces in case of impact on a wide surface, which is one of the reasons why the robots are rounder. They also don't have exposed motors. All these features together reduce or eliminate the need of

fencing and simplify the way we think around safety. It is important to highlight that a risk analysis must be performed as per safety site procedures and all the precautionary measures should be implemented as dictated by TS 15066, and common sense.

- **Simplification of Supervision.** – The role of a supervisor in a production environment is extensive. When a Cobot works autonomously the entire shift gives the supervisor the opportunity to dedicate more time to other opportunities. In that way, having a trustable "co-worker" with no safety or ergonomic concerns providing the same level of quality day after day makes the entire operation better and less need of supervision.
- **Simplification of Investment.** – Funding the purchase of a manufacturing asset in most companies is a long and tedious process that requires many explanations at different levels of the organization. Affordability and attractive return of investment (ROI) make the capital approval process for Cobots less stressful. Demand is going up as well as the number of offerings keeping prices in the $20-$30K range with more and more features and more sophisticated versions. Another factor regularly ignored is the cost of running and operation with industrial robots require engineering skills for programming and maintenance valued high in payroll. Besides all the auxiliary equipment required for safety. Manufacturing is reaching an inflection point at which, it is attractive to invest in Cobots to replace unsafe and tedious manual labor.

Cobots have demonstrated to be useful to eliminate variation out of the manufacturing process; they minimize unnecessary activities at the workstation level, simplify controls, improve productivity by reducing training curves and down times, augment flexibility, and improve product quality in a safe environment. They are as well affordable, safer and easy to use. In brief, Cobots are predicted to simplify more and more tasks; as a result, the level of Cobot implementations will undoubtedly dictate the manufacturing competitiveness of the future.

In the Collaborative Robots and Advanced Vision Conference in San Jose California in November 2017, Rodney Brooks the developer of many successful Cobots such Baxter and Sawyer commented that with the new technologies integrators are going to be out of business. The applications will be so easy to implement and the "coding" so intuitive that no need to pay huge amounts of money to integrate Cobots in the applications such as:

1. **Pick and Place**. - One of the main advantage is when you need to pick from an unsafe location, and place it in a location close to an operator to pick it up in order to continue adding value to the component. Another advantage of working with Cobots is that as your operation moves in your production floor your Cobot can move with it, and there's no need of complicated setups or retraining. The drawbacks are in the cycle times. If you are expecting pick and place parts in the milliseconds you may be disappointed, however if your application requires single digit cycles or more, you are good to go with this technology. Most of the Cobots come equipped with pallet routines, meaning that you don't need to program all the locations in the case the material to be picked or placed required an array configuration. The precision is around (.004 inches). Finally, the most obvious and great feature is the ability to collaborate in a safe environment.

2. **Machine tending**. - Collaborative robots since they can be redeploy can service different machines with a little setup. You can use them for example for a CNC on the first shift and a different machine on the second shift since these type of production are known to be low volume. Once again, preventing the operator to get closer to a machine and eliminating the repetitive tasks are the valued features of this type of applications with Cobots. The other great advantage is that most of the Cobots have external triggers that can be synchronized with the machine, and if you've got the right Cobot with enough degrees of freedom and sufficient cycle time from your application you can even open the door of the equipment. Because of the redeployment factor, you can place the robotic cell in a mobile structure which allows to switch between human operators or Cobots at any time.

3. **Quality Inspection**.- When you can collaborate with a Cobot to preload a pull tester for example, repeating the exactly same technique over and over to increase precision and consistency, your quality inspection cycle time got reduced increasing productivity and because of improvement of repeatability, the opportunity for error is lower increasing quality. Other control applications testing chip quality by picking, inserting and releasing a chip has been successfully accomplished with Cobots as well as delicate touchscreen testing applications with no damaged caused by grasping, swiping, and taping with a pen the screen to accomplish the testing routine.

4. **Assembly support**. - Since you are creating a collaborative environment (Note: remind that all the applications should be submitted to a risk assessment that we'll explain in the following sections), you can support your operation with the Cobot for non-dexterity tasks such screw driving, or others where solvents are used gluing, or welding, snapping parts. Some of the Cobots are equipped with infinite rotation and force control that you can use for screwing applications, some others can maintain constant pressure to ensure consistency when throwing a line of glue for example.

After this quick list of applications it becomes evident of the advantages of the Collaborative robots vis-à-vis of the antecessor the industrial Robots. The inherent safety features embedded into a Collaborative robot solution, the easiness of programming and redeploying, among others make the Cobots a more suitable asset for the factories of the future. A comparative analysis of the old and new generations of robots puts in evidence their impact in manufacturing.

Old Generation (Industrial Robots)	New Generation (Cobots)
Unaware of surroundings. Whatever happens outside its cage isn't considered. You need to feed them with the material they are going to process	It reacts to the environment. It can spring back if collision occurs and has a torque detector to reduce impact.
Compete on precision, speed, and repeatability	Focused on flexibility and ease of use
Dangerous, oblivious of surroundings	Relatively safer
Task must be restructured for that solution	Task done just as a human does it. Some Cobots allow hand guiding routines and optimize from that starting point.
Requires external components, and integration that increase cost	Fully integrated. Out of the box solution ready. No integrator required!
Requires expert programmers. The operational cost is sometimes higher than the initial investment.	The operator in the line can train the robot. The maintenance cost is low or negligible.

The question that you may have at this moment is what makes a Robot collaborative, what are the technologies and concepts embedded in these "machines" that transformed a blind caged robot into an element capable of collaborate. Below is a graphical summary of features to take into account to claim a robot as Collaborative:

Feature	Description and Benefit
Kinematic redundancy	Up to seven degrees of freedom. Single rotational axes number allow the EOT to get into complex fixturing conditions.
Fast Setup and easy re-deployment	A collaborative Robot arm can be repurposed easily for new tasks increasing flexibility of manufacturing schedule. It can be redeployed and integrated into production by the operators
Easy programming	Technical expertise on coding is not necessary to program a collaborative robot for a new task making its integration to the production floor faster and easy
Minimal Supervision	Work autonomously for extended periods of time without supervision increase productivity and quality.
Human like	When designing the application the collaborative robot is similar to a human element since the feeding and exit of material can be accomplish in a small footprint that fits in the line without large infrastructure around
Task Oriented	The collaborative robot isn't focused in executing commands but on accomplishing a task, so if a small deviation occurs, it can still get to its targeted position.
Safe	• Torque sensitive that reduces the harm of a collision if this happens. • Some collaborative robots are equipped with "elastic actuators" that spring back when sensing a collision. • The arm changes from stiff full speed mode into a join impedance mode when it detects unexpected contact with an object or human.

Human- Robot Collaboration

Collaboration is the acting of working with someone to produce or create something. It is difficult then to collaborate when you are in a cage, when you are in prison, when the only way to pass you material to complete the transformation process is through a small window or passing fences and detectors. A visual allegory of an industrial robot is shown in the figure below.

Figure 34 Industrial robot allegory

Industrial robots since oblivious of the surroundings require extensive implementations to place the raw materials inside the cage at the reach of the robot and then similar mechanism to exit the goods. The collaboration in this scenario is limited or none, it is complex and the space around a cell like this becomes a "danger" zone.

One of the reasons for complexity is the lack of standards across the highly fragmented robotics industry. AS mentioned by Samuel Bouchard in his book Lean Robotics: "Robotics standards are like tooth-brushes: everyone agrees we should use them, but nobody wants to use someone else's."[19].

According the international standards ISO TS 15066, there are four types of collaborative features for robots [32]:

Safety and Monitor stop. – This function ceases the robot motion before a human enters into the collaborative workspace[1] to interact with the robot system and complete a task. For example when a part needs to be

---

[1]   Collaborative Workspace.- Space within the operating space where the robot system and a human can perform tasks concurrently during production operation.

handled by a Cobot and a human needs to load it into the end effector or complete a secondary task while the Cobot still handling the part. When the Cobot is in the collaborative space the function is active and the robot stopped then the human is allow to enter and perform the task, the Cobot resume motion as soon as the human has exited the collaboration zone. It is important to notice that the Cobot is not shutdown but motionless (brakes on). One of the advantages of this function is when working with heavy parts requiring human complementation. The main drawback is when the system is located in a heavy traffic area that will stop the unit frequently. The table below resumes the different operation conditions:

Cobot motion		Operator's Proximity to Collaborative workspace	
		Outside	**Inside**
Collaborative Robot proximity to Collaborative workspace	**outside**	CONTINUE	CONTINUE
	Inside and Moving	CONTINUE	STOP
	safety rated monitor stop activated	CONTINUE	CONTINUE

Figure 35 Safety rated and Monitor Stop Function

Hand Guiding. - In this method the operator uses a hand operated device to transmit motion commands to the Cobot. Before the operator enters into the collaborative space to conduct a hand guiding operation the Cobot achieves safety rated monitor stop. Once the operator takes control of the Cobot the safety rated monitor control is cleared. As soon as the operator releases the hand guided device the safety rated monitor is issued. When the operator exits the collaborative workspace the Cobot resumes non-collaborative operation.

Speed and separation Monitoring. - In this method of operation the Cobot and the operator may move concurrently in the collaborative workspace. During motion, the Cobot never gets closer beyond the protective separation distance[2], when the separation distance decreases below the protective separation distance, the Cobot stops. When the operator moves away,

---

[2]   Protective separation distance.- shortest permissible distance between any moving hazardous of the Cobot and any human within the Collaborative space

the Cobot resumes motion automatically according to the requirements of this clause while maintaining at least the protective separation distance. When the Cobot reduces its speed, the protective separation reduces accordingly.

In summary, the position of the operator in this method is detected with Lidars [3] and vision systems. If the operator gets closer, the Cobot slow down, and stops when operator position range is below the protective distance. This is the most common method for the bulk of the applications.

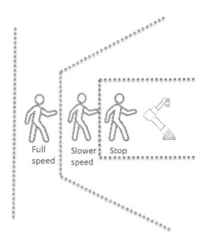

Figure 36 Speed and Separation Monitoring

Power and force limiting. - In this method of operation, physical contact between the Cobot and the operator can occur either intentionally or unintentionally. This is the most worker friendly method since the Cobot can work alongside humans without any additional safety devices. The Cobot senses abnormal forces in its path and it is programmed to stop when it reads and overlaod in the force. Risk reduction is achieved through inherently safety means or through safety related control system, by keeping hazards associated with the Cobot below threshold limits determined during the risk assessment.

The ability of the Cobots to read forces in their joints allows the detection of abnormal forces applied on them while at work. If the Cobot gets in

---

3   Lidar. - Detection system that works on the principle of radar, but uses light from a laser.

contact with a human it can spring back or reverse positon immediately. This means dissipate the energy transferred from the impact.

A summary of type of collaborative operation is shown in the table below:

	Speed	Separation Distance	Torque	Operator control	Risk reduction
Safety rated Monitored Stop	Zero while operator in the Collaborative workspace	Small or zero	Gravity + Load compensation only	None while operator in Collaborative Workspace	No motion in presence of operator
Hand guiding	Safety rated monitored Stop	Small or zero	Ass by direct operator input	Enabling device. Motion input	Motion only by direct operator input
Speed and Separation Monitoring	Safety-rated monitored speed	Safety –rated monitored distance	As required to execute application and maintain minimum separation distance	None while operator in Collaborative Workspace	Contact between robot and operator prevented
Power and force limiting	Maximum determined by risk assessment to limit impact forces	Small or zero	Maximum determined by risk Assessment to limit static forces	As required for application	By design or control, Cobot cannot impart excessive force

Figure 37 Type of collaborative operation

Cobot Market Options

It suffices to surf Internet searching for Collaborative Robots to check on the array of offers. There is a lot of literature on each robot, so the goal of this section is to give you a summation on important specifications to rapidly realize if a Cobot is adequate for the problem you are trying to solve.

The outline includes the model of the robot, the company and a brief description with: The number of axes or degrees of freedom that will help you to get into complex fixtures or nest; the payload the arm can carry without considering the end effector weight; the reach of the robot wrist measured from the base to check the extend of the arm for example when there are fix elements in the station where the robot will be deployed; the speed is an important factor when you need your application to be completed within a specific cycle time; the Ingress Protection (IP) will give you an idea about the degree of protection against intrusion such as dust and water; the total weight of the robot has implications on the way you are going to install it or deploy it; the repeatability is an important specification when dealing with exact locations where the arm needs to place an object, fasten a screw at a specific location and do this task over and over with tight tolerances.

Next is a list of Collaborative Robot solutions for the most known companies and it is by far a non-all-inclusive summary:

Model	Company	Description
	UNIVERSAL ROBOTS – UR3, UR5 & UR10	Axes: 6 Payload: 6.6 lbs. (UR3) Reach: 500 mm Task repeatability: +/- 0.1mm Speed: 1m/sec Weight 24.3lbs IP: 64
	RETHINK ROBOTICS – SAWYER	Axes: 7 Payload: 8.8lbs Reach: 1260mm Task repeatability: +/- 0.1mm Speed: 1.5 m/sec Weight 42lbs IP: 54
	F&P PERSONAL ROBOTICS - P-Rob 2R	Axes: 6 Payload: 3 kg Reach: 775 mm Task repeatability: +/- 0.1 mm Speed: 100°/sec Weight 20 kg IP: 40

AUBO ROBOTICS -AUBO I5

Axes: 6
Payload: 5 kg
Reach: 924 mm
Task repeatability: +/- 0.05mm
Speed: 2.8 m/sec
Weight 24 kg
IP: 54

ABB - YUMI

Axes: 7 per arm
Payload: 0.5 kg per arm
Reach: 559 mm
Task repeatability: +/- 0.02mm
Speed: 1500 mm/sec
Weight 38 kg
IP: 30

FRANKA EMIKA

Axes: 7
Payload: 3 kg
Reach: 800 mm
Task repeatability: +/- 0.1mm
Speed: 2m/sec
Weight 18.5 kg
IP: 30

KUKA - LBR IIWA

Axes: 7
Payload: 15.43 lbs.
Reach: 800 mm
Task repeatability: +/- 0.1mm
Speed: 98°/sec
Weight 23.9 kg
IP: 54

MABI ROBOTICS - MABI SPEEDY 10

Axes: 6
Payload: 10 kg.
Reach: 1384 mm
Task repeatability: +/- 0.1mm
Speed: 120°/sec
Weight 28 kg
IP: 54

YASKAWA -HC10

Axes: 6
Payload: 10 kg.
Reach: 1200 mm
Task repeatability: +/- 0.1mm
Speed: 120°/sec
Weight 47 kg
IP: 20

STÄUBLI - TX2-60	Axes: 6 Payload: 3.5 kg. Reach: 670 mm Task repeatability: +/- 0.02mm Speed: 8.4 m/sec Weight 51.4 kg IP: 65

Autonomous Mobile Robots

AGVs-AMRs are an important enabler within Industry 4.0 paradigm. The automation of the materials flow, from raw materials through to finished goods supports a better and more efficient manufacturing by increasing connectivity and reducing delivery times between the warehouse and production floor. Some benefits are depicted here below:

Automation Technology has transformed manufacturing assembly from high volume faster processes to robotic solutions for an increasingly more flexible production. However, while most of the assembly and testing processes have hugely benefited from automation, materials handling hasn't changed that much. Moving parts from point A to point B appeared to be forgotten by innovators.

It is until the recent business model disruptions triggered by technology giants such as Tesla, Uber, Google, Otto and others that a rethinking of transportation inside a manufacturing facility took place. The conveying of the vehicle market innovations into manufacturing have propelled Autonomous Guided Vehicle (AGV) making it more accessible and Return on Investment (ROIs) more appealing. However, not all models fit the purpose and a close review of your needs should be done carefully.

In the first part, this section will talk about the role of the AMRs in manufacturing as well as to position AMRs in the Industry 4.0 context and the reasons of its potential demand increase. This part also summarizes the inefficiencies related to materials handling; the implications of changing the current human model to an automated model, and the improvements in connectivity, cost and manufacturing velocity.

In the second part, an analysis of the most important specifications needed to correctly choose an AGV/AMR are detailed. Why specifications such as navigation are important? What are the different technologies available? What is the most convenient option for your application?

At the end, this section describes suggests specific AGV/AMR brands the pros and cons as well as to provide some recommendations.

AMR Introduction

At the personal level, you may be entertained by looking an autonomous golf cart that follows you around the course carrying your bag, or pleased to know that somebody with physical disabilities can now increase his/her independence thanks to better mobility technologies with navigation capabilities.

At work you wear your utilitarian cap and observe all the material movement. The natural instinct inherited from years and years of Lean Culture is to connect the processes to increase efficiencies even at the cost of losing flexibility. A new layout is issued, a material handler job standardization is created, the "steps" reduced, and the overall simplification of the material movement and delivery is presented at the closing Kaizen meeting, the change is formalized and the team dismissed.

The above described approach to simplify and reduce waste even prevalent still uses one or several people to move material, however now with a rational sequenced route for the delivery, and for a shorter distance. The inevitable natural next step to solve this persistent inefficiency is to automate the remaining transportation using autonomous vehicles within the manufacturing space.

The leading disrupters are moving ahead with AMR implementations because:

1. A **positive cost benefit** exist either because of large volumes of material require to be moved or the cost of labor provides a positive ROI.
2. **Improve flexibility**. Moving the process location without the human effort associated with it frees up opportunities and creates new efficiencies.

3. The **interaction with the production** environment doesn't require extra investments. The gates to communicate warehouse and different production areas are PLC controlled or the surface across the facility is without abrupt changes in surface. In summary, the implementation into the existing facility will have minimal disturbance.

4. **Ergonomic and Safety** are critical KPIs and moving heavy and bulky material by humans is not a desirable state representing a constant risk and ergonomic detriment.

5. **A long term vision** is in place to use next generation manufacturing tools in combination. For example, Information systems communicate job orders status to the AMR to take direction to deliver material for next order or pick up finish good and take it to the warehouse without need of the robot to be summoned.

Autonomous vehicles may have a slower adoption under certain circumstances:

1. The cost advantage of automating solely the material transportation compared with the current state is marginal especially in economical labor geographies,

2. Facility is to complex and infrastructure for movement of AMRs requires upgrades

3. Site reliable communication such Wi-Fi requires an extra investment

4. Volumes aren't high enough to justify the investment.

The reasons to implement or not are different according to the level of readiness of each facility and such a decision requires an internal review to fairly assess the benefits in the short and long term.

Autonomous Mobile Robots and Manufacturing 4.0

Industry 4.0 as any emergent model has different names, constantly changes, and includes different technologies. AMRs are an important enabler within Industry 4.0 paradigm. The automation of the materials flow, from raw materials through finished goods supports a better and more efficient manufacturing by increasing connectivity and reducing delivery times between the warehouse and production floor. Some benefits are depicted here below:

Operating Cost. - Indirect labor occupied in transporting material between two points is pure *waste*. Looking at making it shorter by relocating operations to connect processes has been the mantra of Lean Manufacturing. AGVs-AMRs offer the opportunity of removing the human variable associated with this operation creating a more cost-effective environment.

Market Forces. - The insatiable customer appetite for choice is growing customization needs, and the shorter life-cycle of products as well as demand for more variety is creating an explosion of SKUs. These market forces increase complexity of manufacturing overall, and consequently of logistics, having a rapid response to deliver the right parts at the right time at the right location is now paramount and becoming more and more important.

Inventory. - From a mere inventory perspective, AMRs support the reduction of the "in transit" material attributed to human labor inefficiencies impacting cash-flows. By transporting finished goods back to warehouse based on automated production completion signals, eliminate waiting times as well as improves space utilization.

Ergonomics. - The result of having an improved logistic from the ergonomic perspective are huge eliminating the lifting and carrying of heavy materials and goods. The risk based on the above assumptions is also impacted.

Internet of Things. - Looking into a non-distance future, machines will autonomously move material through the facility connecting with AMRs to complete this purpose. Transportation of point A to point B will take place as per machine commands of needing more material to complete the production order or because material needs to move into the next value added operation or to the warehouse as finish good.

Now that we are acquainted with the reasons why this technology is disrupting manufacturing, let's take a look into the difference between an AGV and an AMR and most important specifications.

AGV versus SDV or AMR

AGVs (Automated Guided Vehicle) have been moving material around for over half a century. The first AGV, a form of mobile robot, was brought to market in the early 1950s and used in industrial applications to move materials around a factory or warehouse [6]. Over the decades, AGV navigation evolved marginally, with today's AGVs picking up directions from magnetic tape on the floor, fixed reflective markers installed on the walls, or magnetic plugs and bar code stickers strategically placed along the vehicle's pre-programmed path. Their effectiveness, however, is being challenged by a more technologically sophisticated approach: AMR (Autonomous Mobile Robots) or SDV (Self Driving Cars). AMRs are faster, smarter, and more efficient than its grandpa AGV. AMRs are simpler to set up, easier to use, and more affordable.

A guided vehicle follows fixed routes along magnetic tape in the ground. It has simple sensors to prevent collisions (stop) but it doesn't change its route!

A robotic AMR is a much more sophisticated system. It's packed with sensors and powerful on-board computers that help it to understand its operating environment. An AMR can navigate dynamically using a map, allowing it to plan its own paths to travel quickly and efficiently anywhere you want it to go. Adding somewhere new just means expanding the map. AMRs are also smart enough to recognize and react to people, cars, forklifts, and all of those other things that you probably have cluttering up your space. They can also safely continue doing their jobs no matter how busy the surrounding environment.

AMRs use cameras systems, laser sensors, and computer hardware. Automated guided vehicles represent an earlier generation of technology that simply can't keep up with the flexibility and cost effectiveness of autonomous mobile robots.

AGVs and AMRs are often confused even though each system operates with fundamentally different technology, from perception and navigation software to onboard sensors. Therefore, they have different capabilities and potential applications.

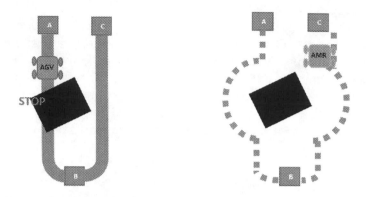

Figure 38 AGV versus AMR

Automated material transport has experienced an evolution due to rapid advancement in sensors and big data capability. Autonomous next-generation solutions are disrupting conventional AGV technologies with 5 core advantages:

- **FLEXIBLE AND VERSATILE**: AMRs do not require external infrastructure for navigation, making implementation hassle-free and highly scalable.
- **EASILY SCALAB**LE: Additional AMRs can be operational in <1 day as they operate from a centrally controlled map, shared among the fleet.
- **REDEPLOYABLE**: AMR can be redeployed from one plant to another, or to a different zone within the same plant. Setup time is minimal.
- **INTELLIGENT**: Onboard intelligence enables AMRs to adapt to changing environments and easily integrate with other solutions (including ERPs). Machine learning collects data and updates the fleet's shared map with learned parameters.
- **USABILITY**: Implementation includes mapping facility once with a vehicle then setting up zones and points of interest on the map in the fleet manager.

How to choose an AMR

At the end, as any other technology AMRs need to fulfil a purpose, an AMR needs to transport and deliver things between two points navigating the intricacies of the facility efficiently and without incidents. I found three important considerations when looking to fulfill this purpose:

Environment: moving from point A to point B it depends as much of your robot as from the environment. You may think that because an AMR can move around alone it doesn't need anything else, this is a misunderstanding, and most of the communications with the robot are made using a reliable Wi-Fi network. At the same time, you need to review physical limitations such as corridors, and steps that will put the robot into an impossible continuation of its trajectory. You need then to evaluate your network reach and your facility spaces to check the robot won't be unable to move from one point to another. You also need to evaluate your floor for imperfections and flatness. Those irregularities can cause a robot to go off track.

Internal features: Navigation, Obstacle avoidance, carrying capacity, ease of use, and battery run time are some of the important features you need to review to determine if the AMR is a good solution for your opportunity.

Social: When multiple autonomous vehicles operate within an area, to achieve high levels of efficiency they require a management system capable of supervising the fleet and interfacing with the environment.

In summary, in order to choose correctly the AMR for your application, you need to review the space where the robot is going to operate (environment), check if your payloads match the robot capacity and the volume of your payload to determine the best platform, double check if the robot's navigation is going to be over complicated or if the planned route deems appropriate as well as all the communication aspects. Let's review some of the internal features:

Payload and Battery Capacity

How much weight your vehicle can move is one of the most important specifications to check prior to look at the price tag. The implications of carrying a weight are several. The framework required by the vehicle needs to be proportional. Robot's momentum depends on the mass and velocity and you can't easily change speed or direction when you load your AMR to the high of its capacity or running at its maximum speed. At the same time, the heavier the load, the larger the friction and lower ability of the vehicle wheels to rotate. The force required to move is higher requiring higher levels of energy lowering battery life.

Standard battery charge time or run time can go from 5 hrs to 10 hrs but it will highly depend on the distance and weight. As important as it is how long it takes for your battery to deplete as it is to recharge since this will keep your vehicle at the dock station for certain period of time. Battery charges depends on the battery technology but a standard charge period can go up to 12 hours.

The payload your AMR will carry is directly related to speed, acceleration, and size of your platform, and impacts your energy consumption. In summary, special attention should be taken to the physics relationship of these factors when reviewing the specifications of an AMR to avoid having your vehicle in the battery dock all the time or to prevent unnecessary risk due to be unable to prevent collisions.

Navigation

Today manufacturing environments are dynamic, the materials delivery is no longer highly predictable, and i.e. a work order can start or be completed at different points on the production floor. As flexibility increases, the configurability of the manufacturing environment increases as well creating different routes for material transport. The obstacles that an AMR will confront are not static and require reliable navigation. There are several types of navigation: tele-operated, semi-autonomous, and autonomous.

Semi-Autonomous

The robot navigates using magnetic tape on the floor or using sensors installed across the path that connects point A with point B. An improved system guides the robot combining tape technology with markers such as colored images around the aisles that a camera on the driverless vehicle recognizes for navigation. Other similar tactics include using magnets and sensors to guide the vehicle. Physical markers and wires are inflexible and often costly. The applications for this type of navigation is on fixed and short routes such as linear corridors. These solutions when in short routes is the easiness of implementation. The main disadvantages is the inability to scale up without cumbersome infrastructure deployments that sometimes interferes with daily production activities.

Autonomous or Natural navigation

Natural navigation means the AMR ability to determine its own position and then plan a path towards its goal location. In order to navigate the environment, the robot requires a representation or map of the environment and to have the ability to interpret that representation. In other words, it needs to create a local map in real time and know how to read it (knowledge base) to determine its position and based on the commands received go to the desire location executing the planned path. See figure below for more details.

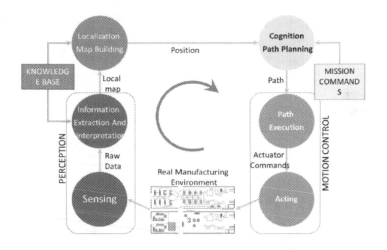

Figure 39 Autonomous Mobile Robot System

Most AMRs use measurements from a LIDAR (Light Detection and Ranging) sensor to recognize natural landmarks such as walls and other surfaces. In other words, to visualize the world around.

To figure out where it is, the AMR matches the information from the LIDAR with the information of location and orientation of objects on its map in real-time. The LIDAR is precise enough that AMRs can detect that they're in one specific aisle, even if your warehouse has hundreds of aisles that are arranged identically. Different solutions using a combination of vision systems and LIDAR are available. Of course an AMR navigation depends on the quality of its map.

The making of this map or knowledge base is a critical task with advantages and limitations. For example, there are restrictions on how much space a single map can cover and it is a critical question to ask to the AMR supplier. If you can cover your entire environment in one map you will be able to use multiple AMR using a single map. Another consideration is how easy is to make a reliable map or how easy is to expand it. These changes should be easy to update using a friendly human interface or amicable software without substantial amount or technical expertise from your AMR manufacturer.

Avoiding Obstacles

This is the most important capability that makes AMRs a much better option than an AGV as explained in previous chapters of this report. Navigate across your manufacturing environment safety and with confidence relies on the combination of multiple sensors to perceive or get a picture of the world. LIDAR has a great range and accuracy, however it can only see in one plane, so the AMR complements its perception with shorter range cameras that can see the areas both close to the ground and above the robot.

Detecting an obstacle is half of the problem, avoiding it is the second half. Once you recognize the obstacle, the vehicle needs to make a correction on its trajectory; so if the obstacle doesn't move, the AMR plans a safe path around it. If the obstacle is a human and it is moving, the problem is more complicated and moving around could lead to a collision. In order to solve this situation, the AMR needs to know where the human is moving towards and make an "intelligent" prediction about his/her motion.

Some of the techniques used to build the algorithms to predict obstacles position are Fuzzy Inference and Neural Networks and it is currently an active field of research and experimentation.

Safety Standards

The **ANSI/ITSDF B56.5 - 2012**, Safety Standard for Driverless, Automatic Guided Industrial Vehicles and Automated Functions of Manned Industrial Vehicles effective since 2013 covers mobile robots, however it is important to highlight that there are gaps that still need to be addressed such the onboard systems (robot arms) and the interaction between ARM and on board robot, who has the stop functions, interlocks, others.

Applications

The fulfillment of the requirements of a specific application using AMR technology goes hand in hand with the level of maturity of AMRs, for example if your requirements are simply to transport material from point A to point B, you may need to deploy basic capabilities of the ARM. These are the capabilities:

Navigation: Is the capacity of the AMR to accommodate for the complexity and variability of the environment on its own. The most common application is simply to carry a load on top of the unit from one point to another using the above described navigation techniques with the size, payload and battery restrictions. In busy warehouses AMRs are amply used to move material from its rack location to a point where a kit is pull together or a purchase order is finalized.

Material Handling: Capability to autonomously handle material. It combines two key characteristics: material transport and material transfer, which relates to the robot's ability to load and unload material to increase the overall efficiency of a process. Some solutions such as the KARIS PRO System can transport and connect with conveyors to form a flexible conveyor. Other systems such as MiR can tow carts and some others pick up entire racks or pallets of material and deliver to a fixed position.

Machine to Machine (M2M) communication: The ability of the robot to communicate multidirectional with other machines and IT systems. A solution of this kind summon the mobile robot to a location until the material is required or until the product is completed to move it to a different location either in the warehouse or inside the production floor.

Unattended management: The degree to which the fleet can manage itself and the ability to handle unresolvable conditions externally. A fleet of robots that can solve potential conflicts on corners, or take decisions on what robot will go to what location depending on proximity and intend, or battery life, etc..

AMR Market Options

In the last AUTOMATE 2017 conference in Chicago almost all the big robotic companies had a proposal for AMR. Here are some of the options available:

1) KUKA Navigation Solution. They claim a fine localization for precise determination of the vehicle position. CAD based object recognition for pick up loads makes KUKA the only solution so far to combine a basic pick up and transportation using this feature. https://www.kuka.com/en-us/products/mobility/navigation-solution

2) FLEX OMNI. - They call its AMR solution Robotic Mobility Platform. It can carry up to 450K or thousand pounds. You can load maps via Ehernet or USB and claim a battery run time up to 24hrs. The vendor claims as well that it is a true holonomic mobile platform. More information can be found at: www.stanleyinnovation.com

3) The LD series of autonomous intelligent vehicles from Omron can carry from 60 to 130 kgs and use scanner lasers for mapping and routing. It reach a maximum speed of 1800 mm per second on the lighter version and 900 mm/sec on the heavier one. The stop position accuracy is 100 mm. Battery run time claims are for 13hrs. Communication is done through standard wiFi. No latching capability. More information can be found at: http://www.ia.omron.com/products/category/robotics/mobile-robots/

4) Mobile Industrial Robots has the MiR100 for a payload from 100-220lbs and a precision of 10 inches from a reference point. The maximum speed is 1.5m/sec and the battery can run up to 10hrs. It communicates via Wi-Fi and Bluetooth. It has a version with latching capabilities called MiR Hook that can pick up and drop off carts. An interesting feature is that the MiR can be operated from a smartphone. More information at: http://www.mobile-industrial-robots.com/

5) Aethon has a smart autonomous Mobile Robot called TUG to deliver racks and carts throughout the facility. The way it works is by lifting the racks so there's no manual loading of the vehicle. The feature that we found the most interesting is the wireless connectivity with other elements such as doors, lifters and others, so it can open doors and get into lifters without human intervention. It can carry 1000 lbs and the battery runs for 10hrs. The navigation is achieved using a real-time Multi LIDAR and it moves at 20 inches per second. http://www.aethon.com/tug/

6) COMAU has the Agile 1500. It can tow a payload, it can connect to a conveyor and transfer a payload, ot can alos lift a load after transportation and it can squeeze under a cart, lift it and move it away. It travels at 1.7 m/s with a maximum payload of 1500kg. The

positioning repeatability is +/- 10mm. The battery runs for an entire shift (we assume 8hrs). http://www.comau.com/EN/

7) Fetch Robotics presented the Freight 500 and Freight 1500. As the name indicates each version can carry 500 and 1500 lbs respectively. The vehicle recharge autonomously and battery run up to 9hrs. It used LIDAR sensors and 3D cameras technology for navigation. http://fetchrobotics.com/freight500-and-freight1500/

8) The self-driving autonomous robots from Otto use laser sensing and Artificial Intelligence to move through the facility. The Otto 100 moves at 2m/s and it loads 100kgs. It lifts 62mm to engage with carts or racks. The battery runs for 8hrs. The Otto 1500 is a version for a 1500 kgs capability. more information at: https://www.ottomotors.com

9) Numerous other small companies are getting into the manufacturing mobile robots market and even though no clear products are marketed a follow up on their technology could add some value. Here some of the companies:
   a. Selftech from Portugal. http://www.selftech.pt/
   b. RoboSoft Service Robots from France. http://robosoft.com/
   c. I am robotics. From USA. https://www.iamrobotics.com/
   d. Clearpath Robotics from Canada. https://www.clearpathrobotics.com/

e.   Bluebotics from Switzerland. http://www.bluebotics.com/
f.   CtrlWorks from Singapore. http://www.ctrlworks.com/
g.   iTEchnic Ltd from United Kingdom. http://www.itechnic.co.uk/
h.   Quimesis from Belgium. http://www.quimesis.be/en/
i.   Symbotic from USA. http://www.symbotic.com/
j.   RIOT Technologies Sp. z o. o. from Poland. http://www.riot.com.pl/

AMR Conclusions/Recommendations

AMRs are going to be another important asset within the manufacturing environment. Taking the time to analyze the fitness of your applications with the multiple options available is the most important step when trying to acquire this technology. The simple review of the ROI is not enough. You need to take into account the state of your facility environment and the reliability of your network signal along the area you're planning to automate. At the same time, the load you are planning to transport and the shape of it is critical. Do you have it in a rack, a cart or it is a box or a bare equipment? Are you going to load the vehicle or are you going to connect it to a conveyor? Are you going to use latching or do you just need a platform? On the area of application you need to review how long the routes are going to be in order to estimate the run life of your battery and the points of recharge. If the recharge is too often, you risk having to take the vehicle to the dock recharging station in a higher frequency lowering the availability of the asset and probably requiring a second unit just because of this. In the payload analysis, you need to ask the minimum and maximum possible load the carrier will take. It is easy to forget these vehicles have limitation and we tend to overload them. This could be extremely dangerous for the vehicle itself and the steering of it and the ability to avoid obstacles.

In terms of options, the market offers a large range of choices with almost all of them similar navigation capabilities differing on payload, battery life and accuracy of location.

Exo-Skeleton Robots

In the 1959 novel Starship troopers of Robert A. Heinlein described wearable suits that augmented soldier's strength, speed, weight lifting, jumping and provided improved senses to the wearer [33]. Since then, the development of wearable robotics intensified by large corporations trying to solve internal ergonomics situations in logistics and manufacturing, the army to provide augmented capabilities to the soldiers and by multiple startup mostly in the medical sector working to provide assistance to persons who are aged, or disabled.

Exoskeletons are mechanical devices whose structure mirrors the skeletal structure of the wearer working in tandem with them, and is utilized as a capabilities amplifier, assistive device, or for rehabilitation. The term exoskeleton comes from nature and means outer skeleton. Many animals, insects, crabs and others have exoskeletons to provide support rather than an inner skeleton like humans do. Exoskeleton technology designed to support manufacturing is now becoming commercially available, and the number of companies introducing these solutions in manufacturing is increasing as shown in the few following examples from the many:

- Daewoo in their shipyards uses suits that helps its employees to lift and move objects that weight up to 66 pounds effortlessly during the three hours battery life [35].
- Ford's assembly workers in U.S. factories are wearing upper body vests as they work on chassis suspended above them. The Vest elevates and supports a worker's arms while the worker is performing overhead tasks, and provides adjustable lift assistance of five pounds to 15 pounds per arm.
- Handful Audi workers at the plants in Ingolstadt and Neckarsulm are testing exoskeletons weighting 6 pounds and many more folks could go bionic in the future if the experiment is a success.

The exoskeleton robot mechanism structures can be classified into the anthropomorphic type, which is designed so that the rotation axis of the robot joint in alignment with the rotation axis of the human joint; the quasi-anthropomorphic type, which has a robot joint functionally similar to the human joint; and the non-anthropomorphic type, which the robot joint is in misalignment with the human joint [34].

The exoskeleton joints can be active, passive, and/or quasi-passive. The power of the robot joints must be generated with active joints such as electric motors or hydraulic cylinders.

Active or passive exoskeletons can also be categorized according to the purpose of muscle strength support: power assistance and power augmentation systems

1) **Power assistance systems** are exoskeleton robots that directly assist power exerted by the human body, thereby giving the wearer greater strength
2) **Power augmentation systems** to amplify the power of wearers, enabling them to perform tasks that they otherwise cannot easily perform by themselves.

In manufacturing, active or passive anthropomorphic exoskeletons are good fits to augment the power of the operator to reduce fatigue and injuries while lifting, move, and holding a weight. The applications go from the transferring of materials in the warehouse, or in the production floor, holding of tools to accomplish a task or a component, piling up boxes, moving heavy components or material across long distances, etc.

The benefits for the wearer are clear as expressed by OSHA who ranks back injuries as the USA number one workplace safety problem [36]. According to the Bureau of Labor Statistics back injuries account for one of every five workplace injuries or illnesses [37]. Furthermore, 33%-41% of all compensation indemnity claims involve back injuries, costing industry $16 billion dollars on top of the pain and suffering borne by employees [38]. Many of these work-related back injuries are caused by frequent, repetitive maneuvering of objects that are not too heavy (fewer than 25 pounds) [39].

From the eyes of the companies promoting the growth of human capabilities to reduce potential harm and improve the well-being of its employees there are collateral benefits impacting key manufacturing metrics that they can collect:

• **Fatigue reduction**. - Repeatedly holding or lifting weights can fatigue the muscles. Inadequate rest periods limits the recuperation preventing the body to recover creating an accumulative effect that impacts turnover, moral, productivity, concentration, etc. Signs of fatigue include drowsiness, moodiness, loss of energy, loss of appetite, and a lack of motivation, concentration and alertness. By wearing the exoskeleton on these operations or activities preserve a good mental and physical shape of the employees.
• **Job function diversity**. - There's no reason why not to increase gender and age diversity on job functions where lifting or carrying is necessary increasing moral and reducing turnover.

- **Less Employees per operation**. - One operation requiring two employees due to the movement of the weight involved maybe reduced to one improving productivity.
- **No more unpleasant operations**. - Rotation of personnel is a requirement on hazardous activities, even though rotation is imperative, looking for volunteers or hiring for that operation can be facilitated if an exoskeleton supports it.
- **Errors reduction**. - The number of errors related to exhaustion and fatigue can be considerably reduced by wearing exoskeletons that decrease overtiredness. The impact in quality will come by a reduction in the number of errors compared to the operation without exoskeleton.
- **Reduction of the pauses**. - When lifting a weight repeatedly, you need to rotate and rest. By wearing the exoskeleton and after a previous risk assessment the operator could extend his/her pauses impacting productivity.

Some limitations of the technology are the weight of the suits that can range from five up to 20 pounds depending on the application and solution, active or passive. Some suits are burdensome to put on and the breaks to go to the restroom could be a challenge. As a note of caution, is important that the introduction of exoskeletons to the production floor or warehouse be accompanied of training and policies determining exactly the limits of weight the operator can lift, hold or carry. The lack of explanation, documentation and deployment of these restrictions can produce the contrary effect.

It exists several uses for anthropomorphic exoskeletons in the industry, however only four are the most common:

- **Back support**. – These are solutions that reduce the forces and torques on the operator (wearer) lower back region cent while he or she is stooping, lifting objects, bending or reaching.
- **Chairless Chairs**. – These are solutions that allow the operator to squat repeatedly for prolonged periods of time by reducing the knee joint and quadriceps muscle forces. The solution has to distinguish between walking, ascending/descending stairs and squatting to allow unimpeded locomotion and only provide support when desired.
- **Tool holding**. - Solutions that reduces gravity induced forces at the shoulder, enabling the user to perform chest to ceiling level task for longer durations and with less efforts. Adjustable sizing allows for natural movement and intuitive awareness of the wearer's position within tight spaces.

- **Power Glove**. - mechanized glove solution that can help workers with a weak grasp gain a stronger hold on tools.

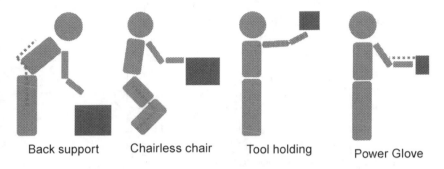

Back support   Chairless chair   Tool holding   Power Glove

Figure 40 Common Exoskeleton uses

There are as well non-anthropomorphic power augmentation systems in manufacturing called intelligent Assisting Devices (IAD). An IAD consist of an electric actuator fixed to the ceiling, or crane that moves a strong wire and a controller. At the end of the wire there is an end effector that grasp the heavy object, or load, and at the same time has a handle for the operator to interface with the IAD to pick up and move the object. A signal representing the operator force is transmitted to a controller, which controls the actuator, the controller assigns the necessary speed to either raise or lower the wire rope to create enough mechanical strength to assist the operator in the lifting task as required [42]. These type of assisting device are common on metal companies, construction warehouse to pile up sacs, rim manufacturing, and others where the location of the heavy movable components don't change over time.

Exoskeleton Market overview

The market of the exoskeletons varies from construction, automotive, even medical. Anywhere considerable weights need to be moved, aligned, lift, and so on, by a human being, an exoskeleton is a good candidate to improve manufacturing. Several companies are looking into this market with specific solution, here some examples:

- In July 2015, the Japanese company Panasonic announced it will begin selling a robotic exoskeleton called the **Assist Suit AWN-03.59** Weighing less than 6 kg, this suit will retail for less than

$9,000 and allow a person to carry 15 kg for up to eight hours on a single battery charge[40].

- SuitX founded in 2011 offers passive solutions for back, leg and shoulder support. **BackX** distributes the weight out of the back into the legs or shoulders providing 30 pounds of support to the lower back (L5/S1). In a study conducted by the University of California in Berkeley it is claimed a reduction of 66% of lower back activation [41]. **ShoulderX** is structure harnessed around the trunk and the shoulders. According to the company in a simulated exercise holding a 1Kg. tool the average holding time increased from 2minutes and 15 seconds to 15 minutes and 30 seconds. **LegX** provides a 60 pounds dynamic leg assistance, in the static chair assistance mode it supports up to 150 pounds.
- **Fortis** is a tool holding passive solution from Lockheed Martin Capable of supporting weight up to 36 pounds. It transfers loads through the exoskeleton to the ground in standing or kneeling positions with no harness around the shoulder or the arms allowing the operators to handle the heavy tools as if they were weightless.
- **Noone** is a Swiss startup that developed a solution for relieving the strain on legs and backs. Its flexible Chairless Chair allows for quick, and easy changes between sitting, standing and walking.
- EksoWorks from Ekso Bionics offers several solutions for tool holding. The **EksoVest** is an upper body exoskeleton that elevates and supports a worker's arms to assist them with tasks ranging from chest height to overhead. The **EksoZeroG** is a Mounted arm leveraging exoskeleton tool holding solution.
- Laevo is a company from Netherlands that offers **Laevo V2** a product that supports your body weight, while you keep your hands free. According to the company, the stresses in your back reduce with up to 40%.
- Activelink, a Panasonic company founded in 2003 developed an active exoskeleton called the Ninja, a full body Power Assist Suit that designed to help lift and carry heavy objects.

Conclusion Exoskeletons

Taxonomy divides Exoskeletons between actives, those using actuators and passive those unpowered. It also categorize those having the human as a model for functioning as anthropomorphic, and it is also explicit between those intended to assist humans on certain disabilities for rehabilitation or better life conditions, and those oriented towards the industry as power augmentation systems to improve ergonomics, safety, Quality, and Productivity. For the passive industrial exoskeletons 4 types were reviewed related to the parts of the body intended to be augmented, shoulder, legs, back, and hands.

The technology continues to evolve into wearable robotics to improve performance by adding lighter materials, more sensing capabilities, more processing data power, and artificial intelligence. An expectation still on the innovation segment of the hype curve as described by Garner Hype Cycle for Emerging Technologies 2017 report [43] is human augmentation where the exoskeleton robots will be a continuation of human physical and cognitive capacities as an integral part of the human body to deliver performance that exceeds normal human limits.

The need for exoskeletons in manufacturing is real, it suffices to look around the facility to realize that innovative solutions are necessary from the warehouse when picking and stocking materials to the production floor to hold tools, move heavy components and so on. Manufacturing then looks to make workers safer and more productive as well as to contribute to their wellbeing. Exo-skeleton aligns to this goal by alleviating the repetitive lifting, moving, grasping, and holding of heavy objects. The adoption by the industry has been slow and it is expected to ramp up as lighter and lighter materials with clever solutions become available at the right price.

Additive Manufacturing

IN THE BOOK Makers, the new Industrial Revolution by Chris Anderson [55], he mentions a story with his grandfather about making an engine out of a block of steel. When he asked, Grandpa, where are the parts? His grandfather answered, inside, we need to pull them out of there. I couldn't find a better example to illustrate what subtractive manufacturing is and how it relies on sculpting parts by machining or cutting. The transformation of the material into a useful component is at this moment achieved by subtracting material to get to the final specification or desired state. By contrast, additive manufacturing adds material layer over layer to complete a part, to form a component. The making of a thing out of an amorphous material has evolved with humanity. These methods have tools that have evolved in parallel with them [64]. For cutting, there are CNC machines that perform a computerized version of cutting, for molding an electric or hydraulic press is used together with a carefully designed mold to allow for flow and cooling patterns, for joining a robot automate the process of fastening objects, and for adding a printer deposits layers of material on top of one another to create an object.

There are multiple advantages on doing additive instead of subtractive manufacturing. The first and most obvious one is the quantity of material used to make a part, there's no removal of material that potential could go to waste, which could be important on certain materials. The second one is the flexibility of going from digital to physical and changing the digital version of your component literally without additional cost. A third advantage is the proximity of the making process. A fourth one is the possibility of achieve structural complexities by adding layer by layer, structures that are impossible to achieve by carving out parts.

In summary, the manufacturing advantages of 3DP are listed here:

1. Reduce overhead Complexity associated with the supply of the low volume component
2. Reduce Supply Risk through Availability of low Volumes
3. Secure lead-time of unique, rare or obsoleted components

4. Reduce lead-time of low Volumes because of vertical integration
5. Reduce cost per unit
6. Reduce number of last time purchases
7. Reduce level of inventory of low volumes
8. Support limited production runs
9. Support Prototypes to accelerate development
10. Support rapid and low cost implementation of jigs and fixtures

Across the life of a product, there is a need to transform digital contextual information into physical tangible material to increase component complexity, increase customer satisfaction, vertically integrate the supply of a component considered at risk, or simply because we want to protect intellectual property by internalizing the production of certain components of our finish good.

The main and bigger goal of Three Dimensional Printing (3DP) in regards to reduce the cost for larger volumes is still out of reach and special attention should be paid to the breakeven analysis. At what volume for what part, it becomes cheaper to 3DP a component than mold it or machine it.

The first and most important aspect when dealing with 3DP strategy is to define the goal. What is the manufacturing reason you want to move into 3DP. The objectives could be varied and need to be aligned with the goals and objectives of your company. The second element is the manufacturing impact you expect to draw out of the implementation of your 3DP goal, i.e. how are you going to measure success of implementation. Then what are the target areas or segments. Finally, the initiative you are going to trigger to achieve that goals. Here are some examples:

OBJECTIVE	IMPACT/MEASURE	TARGETS	INITIATIVE
Reduce procurement complexity	1. Reduction on the man hours dedicated to deal with low volume suppliers. 2. Reduction in the number of low volume suppliers	Eliminate procurement involvement from the supply of low volume 3DP components	Vertical Manufacturing Integration of low volume components

Reduce cost and inventory of low volume components	1. Total 3DP parts cost reduction compared against standard parts.	2. Cost reduction of low volume 3DP parts by 30% 3. One week max of inventory for 3DP parts	Vertical Manufacturing Integration of low volume components
Reduce cost and inventory of Fixtures	1. Fixture developing cycle reduction 2. Reduction of Overall fixture expenses	3. Same day delivery 4. Fixture expenses reduction by 50%	Zero external fixture development
Increase Technology readiness for Additive Manufacturing	1. Number of new products with 3DP components across the entire company 2. Number of 3DP equipment installed across company	1. One final configuration with at least one 3DP component for next fiscal year.	3DP deployment

A 3DP implementation for manufacturing purposes as seem in the above examples, start by defining a clear goal, however not all the areas have been impacted equally. So far, there are three areas for manufacturing where the impact of 3DP in its early stages is noticeable:

- Manufacturing tools and aids: These are Poka-yokes, fixtures and Patter, inspection and test fixtures, Covers, surrogate parts, plugs, drill and saw guides.
- Production Parts for: Market introductions, Limited production runs, Bridge manufacturing
- Rapid Prototyping for: Functional prototypes; Pre-production parts; Form and fit prototypes; Assembly line verification and tuning.

Examples of Additive Manufacturing (AM)

In essence, additive manufacturing is the addition of layers to build up a three dimensional structure from a digital computer-aided design (CAD) file. Additive manufacturing begins with CAD modeling that generates the desired object, the model is sliced in a series of digital images and send to a 3DP machine. The machine uses the descriptions as blueprints to create the item by adding material layer-upon-layer. Hundreds of added layers are assembled until a three-dimensional object emerges. Raw materials may be in the form of a liquid, powder, or sheet and are typically plastics and other polymers, metals, or ceramics

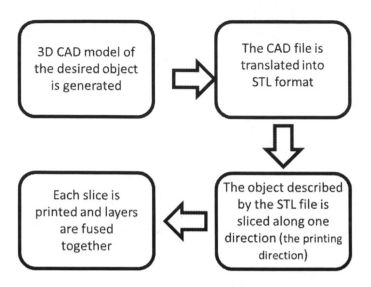

Figure 41 Simplistic View of Three Dimensional Printing

The American Society for Testing and Materials (ASTM) group "ASTM F42 – Additive Manufacturing", developed a set of standards that classify the Additive Manufacturing processes into 7 categories:

1. Photo polymerization. - **SLA** (Stereo lithography)
2. Material Jetting.- **MJ** (Material Jetting); **PJ** (PolyJet)
3. Binder Jetting.- **BJ** (Binder Jetting);
4. Material Extrusion.- **FDM** (Fused deposition modeling); **FFF** (Fuse Filament Fabrication); **PJP** (Plastic Jet Printing)
5. Powder Bed Fusion.- **SLS** (Selective Laser Sintering), **DMLS** (Direct Metal Laser Sintering), **SLM** (Selective Laser Melting)
6. Sheet Lamination.- **LOM** (Laminated Object Manufacturing)
7. Directed Energy Deposition.- **EBM** (Electron Beam Melting), **DMD** (Direct Metal Deposition)

Most of the current additive manufacturing processes introduce some mechanical properties disadvantages such anisotropy (unequal physical properties along different axes), and heterogeneity due to the difference of laser power between the center and the perimeter. These technologies are available for different materials.

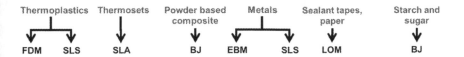

Figure 42 Materials for Additive Manufacturing

SLA (Stereo lithography).

Stereo lithography was the first commercially available 3DP. The principle is a photo polymerization process that uses a laser to cure layer-upon-layer of photopolymer resin (polymer that changes properties when exposed to light). A tray is submerged between 0.002 and 0.006 inches in a basin of liquid photosensitive material depending on the strength of the laser. The laser then traces the pattern of the slice of the CAD model and cures it. The tray after laser completes the layer lowers by a layer thickness. The process repeats until the part is completed. The thickness of the layers can affect the quality of print and tolerances. The laser travels the entire path of the part's cross-section as it builds up each layer, so speed becomes an important consideration. Objects made using stereo lithography generally have smooth surfaces, but the quality of an object depends on the quality of the SLA machine used to print it. The amount of time it takes to create an object with stereo lithography depends on the size of the machine used to print it.

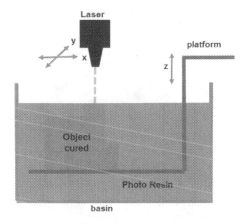

Figure 43 SLA

FDM –Filament Deposition Material

Process using a plastic filament as supplying material. A feeding system pulls the filament into a heater block that melts the material and conducts it to an extrusion nozzle which can turn the flow on and off. The plastic material or resin becomes liquid with the application of heat by the heater block and the nozzle, and solidifies when cooled in the component bed. The object is made by the extrusion of melted material to form layers that hardens immediately after extrusion. This technology is most widely used with two plastic filament material types: ABS (Acrylonitrile Butadiene Styrene) and PLA (Polylactic acid). More than one extrusion or stream is possible. Stratasys has increased up to 500% the build speed by applying a two-axis high speed motion control system that moves each of the two extrusion heads independently. Part quality and accuracy have improved by more intelligent tool path generation software, build strategies and machine control software avoiding overlaps and gaps between adjacent streams of extruded material.

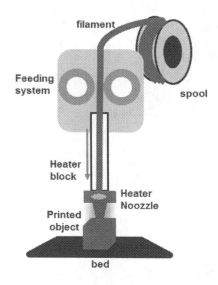

Figure 44 FDM

MJ -Material Jetting Process

Material Jetting is similar to an inkjet printer in that a head, capable of shuttling back and forth incorporates hundreds of small jets to apply a layer of thermos-polymer material, layer-by-layer. Thus, it builds 3D objects by jetting fine droplets of photopolymers, materials that solidify when exposed to UV light. Although photopolymers are a different class of plastics than the thermoplastics and elastomers used in many production environments, they can simulate those materials mechanically, thermally and visually

Wax Material jetting machines utilize inkjet print heads to jet melted materials, which then cool and solidify. By adding layer on layer, the part is built. Wax materials are used with this technology. Material jetting requires support structures for overhangs, which is usually built in a different material.

Binder Jetting (BJ) Process

A binder jetting machine will distribute a layer of powder onto a build platform. A liquid bonding agent is applied through inkjet print heads bonding the particles together. The build platform will be lowered and the next layer of powder will be laid out on top. By repeating the process of laying out powder and bonding, the parts are built up in the powder bed.

Binder jetting does not require any support structures. The built parts lie in the bed of not bonded powder. The entire build volume can therefore be filled with several parts, including stacking and pyramiding of parts. These are then all produced together. Binder Jetting works with almost any material that is available in powder form.

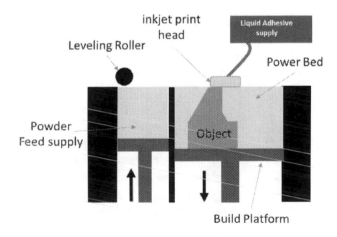

Figure 45 Binder Jetting

SLS - Selective Laser Sintering

Somewhat like SLA technology Selective Laser Sintering (SLS) utilizes a high powered laser to fuse small particles of plastic, metal, ceramic or glass. During the build cycle, the platform on which the build is repositioned, lowering by a single layer thickness. The process repeats until the build or model is completed. Unlike SLA technology, support material is not needed as the build is supported by unsintered material.

A layer of powdered material is carefully laid down by a leveler or roller on the build tray. A laser then sinters the cross-section of the part. Subsequently, the tray drops another 0.002 to 0.004 in. (0.05 to 0.10 mm) and the process repeats. Similar to SLA, layer thickness varies based on laser strength, material, or tolerance desired.

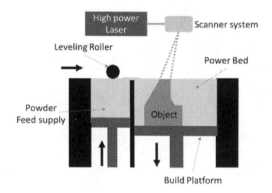

Figure 46 Selective Laser Sintering

LOM –Laminated Object Manufacturing

LOM is a less known 3DP manufacturing process where the object is created by a stack up of layers of paper bonded with heat and pressure. In LOM, paper from feeding roll is the stacked and bonded to the previous layer of paper using a heated roller. The roller melts a plastic coating on the bottom side of the paper to create the bond. The profiles are traced by laser system. The process generates considerable smoke and a localized flame so it requires to exhaust smoke from a sealed chamber. After cutting the geometric features of a layer, the excess paper is rolled in a waste paper roll for disposal. The build platform drops down the thickness of one layer, new material is pulled across the platform and the process is repeated.

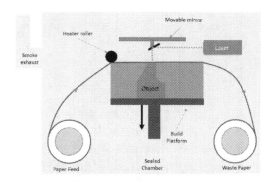

Figure 47 Laminated Object Manufacturing

EBM -Electron Beam Melting

EBM uses a high power electron beam that generates sufficient energy to melt a metal. EBM process takes places in vacuum and at high temperature, resulting in stress relieved components with material properties better than cast. The 3DP machine consists of a nozzle that deposits metal powder or wire on a surface and an energy source electron beam melts it, forming a solid object.

Powder base systems lays down successive layers of powdered material. These layers are melted together using an electron beam that trace the sliced 3D model to build up the parts. This method produce fully dense metal parts directly from metal powder.

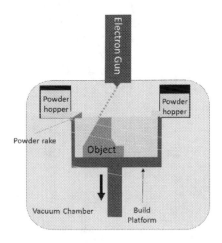

Figure 48 EBM Powder Base System

The metal wire systems use the electron beam to melt a welding wire onto a surface to build up a part.

Cost-Benefit Analysis

The reason why 3DP is the great disruptor is not only based on the free complexity it conveys but in the significant entrance of multiple players to the market and the growing experiences collected by several industries already applying these technologies. Gartner predicts for example, that by 2021, 75% of new commercial and military aircraft will fly with 3DP engine, airframe and other components, 25% of surgeons will practice on 3DP models of patient prior to surgery, and 20% of the top 100 consumer goods companies will use 3DP to create custom products. All the organizations are already working on the cost-benefits and trade-offs where 3DP makes sense compared with traditional manufacturing technologies.

When the initial investment is too high to manufacture few pieces with traditional methods, 3DP could be a good option to examine. Initial investments on 3DP are by far lower than traditional manufacturing, however as the volume goes up the cost per unit for molded, casted or machined parts goes down while for 3DP goes up due to the lack of capacity for larger volumes and the necessity of having multiple equipment to attain such volume. Between these two models exist a cross over point or breakeven point where the cost of making the parts either using 3DP or molding cost the same. A unit cost analysis based on volume to calculate the cross over point provides a good framework to decide to invest on 3DP or not, however a pure cost analysis don't show the intangibles explained in this chapter such as flexibility, complexity free design and others.

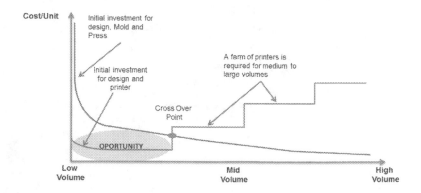

Figure 49 Breakeven analysis

Thus, as the volume increases the opportunity for 3DP weakens. In order to palliate the volume effect, the use of 3D printers in parallel to manufacture parts rapidly is gaining traction to explore opportunities beyond the cross over point. A farm of printers will maintain complexity, flexibility, and eliminate indirect expense related to design of molds while at the same time providing a better cost benefit scenario.

3DP Farm Concept

The number one reason for the low adoption of 3D printing is the long cycle times of the current solutions. This lack of capacity increases the cost per unit substantially keeping molding as leading choice for medium volume and even some low volume production needs. The main roadblock is to have a machine model that carries intrinsic capacity limitations. If instead we convert it into a business model like a farm that we can harvest and offer to internal customers it will help us to overcome capacity limitations and reduce the cost per unit.

A 3DP business model reduces supply risk on parts or components for EOL products, occasional products, and more importantly internally secure the procurement of low and medium volume critical parts by vertically integrating.

The 3DP farm can be allocated to a center of excellence servicing a group of facilities instead of locally purchasing 3D printers. This will provide specialization of the resources, and standardization of the technology.

Such additive manufacturing farm can work on demand basis with minimum volume order sizes, and be scalable with predicted costs:

1) **ON DEMAND.** - Since specifications are digital parameters, orders can be placed anytime, from anywhere. The number of printers available in the farm determine your capacity, so you can estimate delivery time and keep your customer happy.

2) **LOWER INITIAL COST.** - The high initial cost for molding solutions for a particular part gets diluted as the number of units produced increases. So you are prone to go for the larger volumes even when demand isn't there to sustain your claims. In a 3D printing farm your initial cost got is much lower and it increases in steps over time as your volume increases. You don't need to disburse large sums of money from the get go as in traditional methods.

3) **ONE FARM, MULTIPLE PARTS**. - The ability to switch over and over between different works orders on the same asset (printer) without additional investment translates for a 3Dp farm in a reconfiguration to produce different type of parts without increasing the initial cost (no more investment). I can move from part A to part B without further investment increasing the capacity of the farm.

4) **SCALABLE**. - The customer can order a couple units, complete some design reviews and order later a 10 times larger volume with a simple click. A traditional method can't scale without further investment, development and other validation associated costs. A farm of printers can scale immediately if capacity is available.

5) **FREE COMPLEXITY**. - As mentioned before the advantages of this technology are the possibility of having more complex components at the same cost price than noncomplex components. The elimination of down the stream manufacturing cost associated with the assembly of multiple molded parts is another large advantage often forgotten.

3DP farm Assumptions

It is assumed that running a farm is a 24/7 activity. Since we need to lower costs we need to maximize the three pillars of cost:

Material: moving from single printing to medium volume printing will require more plastic that can be negotiated. Now, the prices for the 3DP materials such plastic rods is approaching those of the plastic pellets used in molding, however special attention to consigned resins should be paid.

Assets utilization: Printers return of the investment depends on the number of printers in the farm and the number of parts printer by it, so the driver to impact a low cost per unit is to maximize utilization and lower defect rates. There are two ways to maximize utilization. The first one is by arranging the maximum number of parts per printer run, and the second one is by reducing harvesting and material feeding shutdowns. The overhead cost such energy and indirect personnel should also be considered.

Labor: There are several activities for the operator working in a 3DP farm:

- Harvesting is one of the critical ones, it goes hand to hand with the utilization maximization, in this scenario the operator needs to know what is the next printer that needs harvesting. The big challenge of the farm concept is to convert this process into a more intelligent, and automatic one.

- Material feeding is a critical operation that consumes labor. Depending on the technology the operator managing the farm needs to refill material, or change spool and prevent printers shutdowns due to lack of material. A simple dashboard with the calculation of the remaining material will prevent the operator to make unnecessary tour to check on material availability.
- The other operation is sort and trim, remove the scaffold and trim the part is crucial for a good quality part, it requires human abilities that hardly can be automated, so a good design of the run (or plate where all the parts are arranged) is very important not only to minimize material consumption but to facilitate trimming.

The way a 3DP farm works is depicted in the figure below. The customer send a 3D model from anywhere in the world. The farm technician validates the parametric model and convert it into a STL file. At this moment, the feedback to the customer is provided in terms of feasibility (printers have an envelope or 3D space that determines the maximum size of a printed part). The other activity performed by the technician is to arrange the plate to maximize. The order is then assigned to a parcel or printer in the farm.

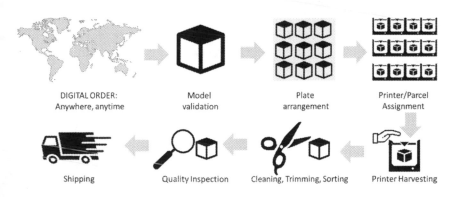

DIGITAL ORDER: Anywhere, anytime   Model validation   Plate arrangement   Printer/Parcel Assignment

Shipping   Quality Inspection   Cleaning, Trimming, Sorting   Printer Harvesting

Figure 50 3DP Farm Process Sequence

The printer or printers complete a unit so a signal of completion is emitted or transmitted for the operator to harvest it or replenish material if necessary. The plate is then moved to cleaning and trimming, then sorting to conciliate work order and component to finally get to final inspection and then shipping.

3DP Conclusions

The future of 3DP is real, tangible and hits old manufacturing pains from product complexities impossible to achieve by traditional methods to shorten of the supply chain but above all it provides a clear path to move forward with the increasing diversity of product configurations that are inundating manufacturing with low volume requirements. It is undoubtedly a game changer in terms of different business models and a business retainer for manufacturers not ready to spend large sums of money on molds for prototypes, small runs or configuration variations.

This chapter presented a simple and direct strategy for you to prioritize different areas of manufacturing depending on your needs and also review some of the basic techniques of 3DP that are currently in the market. We also presented an innovative model to deal with the economics of running mid volume parts that relies in farming printers. This concept isn't exclusive to 3DP and be used for other technologies such farming machining, or farming computer processing, etc.

Humanity 4.X

THIS SECTION HAS the purpose to provide a quick overview of humanity's interactions, impact and change related to the use of emergent technologies. Technology can't be conceived without humans and humans can't be what they are without the support and leverage of technology. This symbiosis have gone through peaks and valleys for centuries, some of the valleys caused by human dogmas, some peaks caused for the mastering of technology. At the end, human and technology are becoming one with the innocuous acceptance of larger pools of everyday life technology enablers. We don't conceive the present without certain technology elements and even though most of the time these enablers have a positive impact, there are nefarious uses of technology that have brought humanity to the border of extermination, like the nuclear arms proliferation.

In manufacturing sites, humans are all around, they interact with robots, sophisticated equipment, manage software platforms, program routes for AMRs, or wear exo-skeletons to prevent injuries. In summary, we live day after day the technology in manufacturing and the interaction with it seems innocent and harmless, however siting around thinking that all is anodyne, that everything works and will work perfect without human intervention is a serious error. This new manufacturing scenario requires a different set of cognitive tools or education, a different type of leadership, and a deep understanding of the environmental impact. In summary human changes constantly and in order to strive in the industry 4.0 era, humans requires to change into a new mindset to co-habit with technology and take the best out of it.

After being talking about Manufacturing 4.0 concept through previous chapters in this book and its technological elements, it is imperative to talk about the collateral effects in humanity, other human-technology-human dependencies, and its environmental impact. In this section, we'll talk about Humanity 4.X in four different significant aspects:

- Education
- Leadership
- Sustainability

Education

The impact of new technology implementation in education is huge as well as the impact in the new profession job descriptions. Who would imagine that a university will offer courses to be a pilot of drones that can support the increasing transportation industry propelled by the internet purchasing exponential increase? Did you imagine yourself working from your house piloting a drone to fertilize fields without being there avoiding chemical exposure? Daniel Pink in his book a whole new mind [66] explain the six essential senses that will make the difference in the future, he explain that teaching our left brain the axioms and algorithms that a computer will master faster, cheaper and better isn't a bet for the future, that we need to think with our right side of the brain as if we were directing an orchestra. The transposition of right brain competencies to a school curricula hasn't been completed yet because of multiple factors such the large social and economic inequality between the countries, and individuals.

Technology made its way into the classrooms. In the past, a lecture used to have a teacher lecturing from a podium while the students siting in the auditorium simulated they were paying attention. Today's classroom has moved to a new stage where the use of new technologies like laptops, tablets, or smart phones instead of books and notebooks is the method that most of students at 21st century take the lessons.

In other words, technology has profoundly changed education. It also expanded access to education by the use of massive amounts of information (books, audio, images, videos) available at the fingertips through the Internet, and opportunities for formal learning are available online worldwide through On Line University Degree Programs, YouTube, podcasts, and more.

Traditionally, classrooms are now isolated entities with limited collaboration. Technology enables forms of communication and collaboration undreamt in the past. Your location no longer matters to attend a lecture or to pass a course or a training. In manufacturing, training is one of the elements with huge impact by augmented reality and web based course, the reduction of travel cost has considerable effect when looking at education options for your employees. A great example is the way AT&T created together with Udacity online training programs for its employees and link them to incentives at work.

Other good example of the technology impact in education is that students can now read scientists' blogs, access to online articles, e-mail questions or talk live with the scientists via videoconference. Students can share not only within the same classroom but all around in an interconnected world.

Technology has also begun to change the roles of teachers and learners. In the traditional classroom, the teacher is the primary source of information, and the learners passively receive it. This model of the teacher as the "sage on the stage" has been in education for a long time, and it is still very much in evidence today. However, because of the access to information and educational opportunity that technology has enabled, in many classrooms today we see the teacher's role shifting to the "guide on the side" as students take more responsibility for their own learning using technology to gather relevant information. From elementary schools to universities across the world, almost everybody is redesigning learning spaces to enable this new model of education with more interaction and smaller work groups using technology as a higher level of education enabler.

Educational apps, search engines, videos, portable technologies, and interactive games provide students with a nearly endless supply of information and resources 24/7. The benefit is the extension of education beyond the regular hours and the possibility of a continuous education by integrating technology to learn at a rate that is comfortable to students. The following concepts are the most significant ones to understand technological impact in education:

1. **Active engagement**. - Technology is interactive, and students learn by doing, researching, and receiving feedback. This helps students become passionate about what they are learning. Imaging having the opportunity of wearing Virtual Reality googles to surf the world searching for adventures while learning geography making a robot following instructions provided by a set of augmented reality lenses. The speed of learning technologies such as molding, machining and others that require a mix of practice and theory will go up. A trend of DIY (Do It Yourself) is inundating the world, the accessibility of tools such Arduino, Raspberry and others as a result of cheaper and better electronics is exploding the number of applications and increasing the engagement for the better of future technology applications in manufacturing and elsewhere.

2. **Use of real-world issues as a model**.-The immediacy of the information provided by the Internet, allows to create models with real data, and generate solutions to real problems. If thinking out of the box is a principle to find solutions for a problem, expanding the box creates a similar and more impactful effect to

3. **Simulation and modeling.** - Simulation development has brought unimaginable environments in front of the eyes of the students for them to play with that environment. For example it allows to check on process flow bottleneck situations and solve them without moving a physical piece of the production floor layout. They provide an important tool for the learning process since the possibility of creating similar to reality scenarios is limitless. Simulation tools for mold flow, parametric design, Finite element Analysis, Process optimization, Design for manufacturing and so on are now part of the curricula of Universities facilitating the integration of those future engineers into manufacturing.

4. **Discussion and debate boards, forums, and working groups.**-You don't know what you don't know until you know that you don't know…and look for a forum where that thing you don't know is explained. Virtual communities for specific manufacturing topics are available for you to check if your situation was addressed by somebody else already. The working groups provide as well a certain level of mentoring and help the manufacturing novices to speed up their learning curve. If you are an experienced manufacturer or engineer in a field and you want to contribute to a larger community, web apps such as LinkedIn are good platforms to give back and be retributive. Online communities also present the opportunity for students to interact with others around the world.

Learning the manufacturing of the future require a whole new set of concepts and a mix of practice and theory to create expertise before going into the real world. The digital revolution, the intensification of the Robotization and the introduction of additive technologies into the manufacturing scenario is creating a gap on current and traditional scholar system. Initiatives to close this gap are launched by entities such the DMDII (Digital Manufacturing and Design Innovation institute) in Chicago.

Having a degree is more than a social expectation, it needs to provide the minimum set of cognitive and hands-on tools to address issues at work. Education with the input of the industry is then responsible of describing curricula and profiles for the next generation of graduates. As we can see now the curricula for an industrial engineer changed couple decades ago introducing topics related to six sigma and lean manufacturing and now needs to adjust again to the reality of digital and automated manufacturing. The majors will change so you can now study to be an automation engineer, or a digital designer, etc. Whatever your professional profiles is, no career is untouched by the industry 4.0 from a lawyer dealing with technology patent to doctor dealing with the use of innovative technological tools all professions are experiencing a transformation. These are some of the transformations:

1. **Hybrid careers**. Who have ever tough about having a social worker following his teams in social media or using software tools to connect and improve his communication or who could have thought a marketing person using augmented reality and web based technologies as they use pervasively now? The use of robots in the OR (Operating Room) is increasing and the knowledge of medicine and robotics is now increasing. Health care careers for example will have more interaction with information systems technologies, augmented reality, virtual reality, and on line collaboration. The mix of social majors with technology is inevitable and the expectation is for this hybrid majors to flourish and generate a new social mindset.

2. **Merged Engineering Careers.** - Take the example of a Mechatronics major which merge the fields of Electronics, Software and Mechanics. The smart combination of different engineering majors is a huge demand of the industry that requires engineers to deal with the higher levels of automation and robotics at the plants. More merging engineering fields are generating new majors.

3. **Art careers** are the ones to be less impacted by the wave of automation and artificial intelligence. There is an increasing need for people capable of exploiting the right side of the brain to solve new problems, orchestrate activities where coordinating people is a necessity or finding new and innovative ludic ways to spend humanities time.

As mentioned before the manufacturing engineering profiles are also suffering a substantial revamp with introducing of new topics that will help students to deal with the new realities of supply chain and logistics to the automation in the floor and the complexity of equipment used for the transformation of materials into finish goods. The capacity to reconfigure our cognitive tools through education in order to deal with a more complex manufacturing environment will distinguish high performers from poor performers.

Leadership

Mark Benioff, the founder of Salesforce said in the World Economic Forum in Davos: we are in a leadership crisis. We are not in a technology crisis [67]. The changes occurring a fast pace in multiple domains for nanotechnology, genetics, Artificial Intelligence, Robotics to name a few require new policies, different legal frameworks and open mind to lead the change.

At the manufacturing site level, leaders face constant changes from the decision on engaging with a supplier using digital tools to the way to approach new ways to improve productivity or innovative ways to track product quality behavior using automated data collection, and so on. The setting is changing, and trying to maintain influence through high level of knowledge is no longer an option or at least it is a very difficult one to sustain. This type of leadership where the authority either manager or supervisor was the one who knows everything is no longer viable. Influence is now a representation by the ability to adopt the change and the way your organization exploit that change to create higher levels of safety, productivity and quality. The expectation is no longer to master and show your technical prowess but to lead and inspire to create the factory of the future. New leaders must recognize the value of technology applications and the purpose to use them. The lack of this awareness can put companies in jeopardy and convert them in laggards. C-suite that understand the benefits that Industry 4.0 brings to the table will reconfigure the organization to adapt to this change by aligning goals and objectives to create new products but also to align the expectations in terms of new pools of profitability and higher levels of product reliability.

A level 5 leader as described by Jim Colling in his book Good to Great [68] have a combination of fierce resolve and humility. In the new manufacturing scenario a level 5 leader should have the courage to pursue ambitious technological initiatives and the humility to say: I don't know but let's try it when presented with technical solutions. However at the same

Performance assessments for employees will change as well as training and career plans where leaders will offer transparency for team members. Competences, skills and talent potential will weight higher on the assessment than traditional 360 feedback techniques based on social perception.

A long road still ahead when dealing with leading a group of people or an organization that constantly lives technology and with a world that doesn't stop to change. The definition of the qualities of those leaders are still in definition stage, however we can note that will require openness to deal with the unknown or not fully proven, courage to move ahead using technologies for manufacturing where nobody has used them before, inclusion to make everybody part of the change and inspiration to be authentic in order to inspire and motivate a vision where technology plays a role.

Sustainability

The importance of having a transformation process that minimize the negative environmental impact is a moral obligation. The use of new technologies brings a lot of benefits but at the same time impacts the environment. The human impact on environmental systems is entering a period of unprecedented change [69]: Greenhouse gases levels not seen for at least 3 million years, earth's biodiversity at mass extinction rates, deforestation rates with wide consequences for the earth's atmospheric circulatory systems, oceans pollution with unprecedented impacts on corals and fish stocks, retreating glacial ice fields, Nitrogen from fertilized dumped into the oceans affecting the fish stocks creating dead zones and impacts on the water cycle creating shortfalls of freshwater.

At the urban cities the impact is also noticeable. The use of digital technologies such as Uber for example that at first glance looks harmless, is exacerbating traffic jams increasing pollution. When sharing our vehicles to transport other people from points A to points B and making some money on the way, we are augmenting the already excessive number of vehicles in the street that for cities like San Francisco translates in chaos, and longer commutes. Technologies such 3DP are moving plastic residuals to areas where people doesn't know what to do with them, and the intensive use of mobile tools such as smartphones, tablets and others are creating a source of chemical contamination of gargantuan proportions. The innocent exponential increase of online purchasing is great for the consumer but translates into more vehicles in the streets to deliver the goods and large quantities of card boxes that are useless after delivery that end in trashcans.

The power consumption due to technology has increased in the last years with all our electrical gadgets working day and night all seasons, televisions, smart phones, tablets, laptops and other devices consumes high levels of energy and the supply for this demand is impacting our environment more than ever. Additionally, these gadgets end in our landfills creating additional contamination.

Figure 51 electronic waste

Beyond the activism to change policies and the necessary debates to reshape mindsets to build sustainable, resilient and better ecological systems. There are some easy behavioral changes we can start as individuals: Think about technologies that you can reuse and recycle, be honest on the impact in the environment of the manufacturing technologies you are proposing.

Technology deployed in manufacturing is the culprit of some ecological disasters, however is also a potential solution to countermeasure the impacts. For example, IoT tools allow for the manufacturers to monitor and control greenhouse emissions, advance materials are now becoming available for batteries that will outperform combustion engineers reducing oil consumption, smart manufacturing facilities use less energy, and toxic residuals are closely monitored to prevent spills. The use of bio based plastics to replace metal and plastic components is gaining traction in automotive sectors. At the same time, the use of robots for remanufacturing are being tested enabling circular economy. In the electronics industry green materials and green materials have a potential to drive environmental benefits by reducing the dependence on toxic material and by reducing the use of water and energy required for the fabrication of packaging material.

The fight for a better and sustainable environment is far to be over, however we have shown that technology rests in both sides of the equation. From one side, it pollutes and disturbs our ecosystem by its deployment, and on the other side, it can be used as the tool to countermeasure the negative effects. While the opportunity to boost your operation by the use of technology will present to all the leaders, the decision to use it or not, is and will continue to be taken by humans, thus the importance of awareness and honesty before profit and revenue.

Topics for further reading

WHEN WRITING A book time collapses and topics evolve or are out of the scope of the writers at that specific moment. In this section, we recognize some of the manufacturing technology trends and important conversation points that should be addressed but they weren't. We expect these technologies to be forces of major impact in the future of manufacturing.

The first and considered the most important threat to the manufacturing digitalization efforts relates to the **cybersecurity**. In the same way a CAD file can be shared almost instantaneously, it can also end in the hands of the competition if the company is the target of a hacking attack. It can be any type of important information, a patent, or a unique assembly process. In the same way you provide access to providers and integrators to prevent production line shutdowns, a cyber-attack can put you out of business for a while if deterrent measures and policies are not in place. Most of the efforts related to Cyber Security are concentrated on protecting the ERP systems and it is important, however the threat of disrupting an operation through the accessing of production access is an unacceptable risk that requires to plan ahead and strategize, allocate sufficient budget and implement countermeasures to reduce risk. The most known type of attack is the one perpetrated by a malicious code such the Trojan, mydoom and others transmitted through email. These viruses keeps your files hostage or overload the traffic to your servers until they crash. The impact in manufacturing is the inability of using certain tools required to complete the manufacturing process. Other type of cyber-attacks are malicious sensors implanted in order to collect data and that can be activated remotely causing the manufacturing asset where they are installed to crash. This important topic will be even more relevant with the exponential increase of IoT applications and the ubiquity of connectivity.

Blockchain is a digital ledger technology used to store and record transactions usually associated with Cryptocurrencies. Blockchain can securely and in a more transparent way, store transactions and records along distributes nodes in a network. One of the potential applications is in supply chain where every product is registered on the Blockchain registry with a unique ID. Each supplier updates information on the product as it moves along the manufacturing process. At each point, the product is scanned to prevent that alternate materials are used, or unauthorized sub-contractors were employed. 3DP technology as explained in this book starts with a CAD file that is sliced then send to the 3D printer to be converted into a physical object. The sharing of these CAD files is performed manually, no traces, tracking the origin, uses, and changes is possible. For example, the files to print a gun are openly available and there is no way to trace back the manufacturing of such dangerous objects. A Blockchain system provides an automatic audit trail of the digital files and enables the track and trace of the asset used to print it. As a nascent technology, the applications will multiply in the future and a clear understanding of the impact in manufacturing is Important.

Warehouse Management Systems (**WMS**) are the software platforms used to control and supervise warehouse operations from the time raw material arrives into the docks until it leaves the warehouse to go to the production floor or somewhere else. WMS provides visibility on the inventory at any time and location. The benefits of using these type of software platforms are countless and they will be even more in the near future due to the complexity increase and the explosion of configurations. At the same time, the combination of technologies such RFID and scanning with WMS facilitates the storage, and picking of the material out of the right location faster than traditional methods. The introduction of fleets of Autonomous Vehicles transporting material from the warehouse back and forth autonomously requires a trustable system to confirm location of the material.

A big absent on this book is **big data**. Even though we recognize its impact in operation analytics, we separated the capturing of the data from sources such MES, ERP and IoT from the manipulation of that data by analytic techniques, or its use in training Neural Networks for inspection purposes. The exploitation of big manufacturing data certainly poses a challenge for organizations looking for efficiencies and ways to take more and more data driven manufacturing decisions. However, harvest more manufacturing data as a goal does not impact a metric or improve an activity. So the emphasis should be in the tools to manipulate the data not in the data itself.

When thinking in manufacturing, probably **drones** is not a technology that comes first to your mind in terms of applications. However, due to the increasing popularity of these artifacts, some applications are starting to be developed on large facilities to surveille and inspect large pieces of equipment deployed across the facility and to automatically replenish material on large machine feeders. Another incipient applications is the combination of drones with RFID technology to measure inventory levels. We are confident that more and more applications will rise with this technology as time goes by and people get familiarized to see them around at work.

Manufacturing will continue to face the dilemma of using or not rapidly accelerating manufacturing technologies, however the major impact will come from their interaction and combination. A production system that is really interoperable because it connects all its assets, software platforms and product is more advantageous than trying to exploit a specific technology. An asset that takes production big data coming from an automated data collection system, and digest it using an artificial intelligence algorithm to really be autonomous is highly more efficient than trying to promote individual production management software tools. WMS platforms that connect with MES platforms to dictate the production plan to all the assets in production, and use AMRs to dispatch material depending on the scheduling is high more advantageous than simply try to exploit new applications of MES or WMS. The use of robotic technologies to harvest a 3DP farm to increase efficiencies and improve the return could be a better option than simply try to look for more and more products to be transferred into a 3DP manufacturing. In summary, the disruption on the manufacturing models will come by the intensive use and collaboration between the different technologies more than by the single exploitation.

General Conclusions

MANUFACTURING COMPLEXITY IS the enemy reducing profit margins of many companies. It comes in different flavors and from different sources, it can be an exponential increase on the routing steps or components in a bill of materials or extremely complicated features in the product. The consequences in cost, quality and delivery so far contained with the strict application of Lean Manufacturing methods is no longer sustainable. A long this book we claim that a set of tools called technology enablers can be applied to handle complexity together with current lean methodologies.

The hype of industry 4.0 and its derivative technologies inevitably created and is creating new business models that improve customer satisfaction, loyalty, and generates new revenue streams but it also significantly impacts key process indicators. These technologies development, integration, use and exploitation which ultimate goal is to improve operations are baptized as manufacturing 4.0 concept that is encircled in a larger concept called Industry 4.0. So, it is not a new concept or new lingo is simply the right framing of the tools out of Industry 4.0 used and applied in manufacturing.

The different technology enablers modify manufacturing positively. In order to facilitate the analysis and the review of their impact, we divided them in three pillars, a sort of adjectives for manufacturing. The first one, **digital manufacturing**, comes from the maturity of digital tools used to manage information rising from the production floor. The second one, **automated manufacturing**, comes from the maturity of automation elements such as robots for specific task previously negated for the lack of enough safety, autonomously, intelligence and simple as better products coming out of a process of further innovation. The third pillar is what we call the **additive manufacturing**, which is promise to be the next big idea to shake manufacturing by simplifying supply networks, and increase product complexity.

Once the manufacturing modifiers comprehended, we outlined a manufacturing 4.0 implementation Strategy as part of the continuous improvement journey to assess, outline solutions, evaluate the benefit and risk, review with stakeholders, and create a portfolio. The purpose is to have a roadmap that provides a guideline to the plant or site on the initiatives to consider to improve the operation and plan ahead for the budget and resources. We also provided explanations of the different technology applications in order to use it as a reference. The goal is for you to have a roadmap to apply these technology enablers on the right problems, the pain points that are holding the operation in order to benefit your organization.

The use of manufacturing technologies is inevitable. It needs to be understood in a larger context than simply return on investment. It is attracting new young talent into a modern company, a company that understands and exploits efficiently what these young engineers use in their daily lives. This is real, the sustainable and measureable success won't come magically after executive orders. All leaders need to understand that the changes aren't optional, and is either change or die later by inaction. In the last section, we discussed the change of mentality on the leadership to adapt to this changes. It isn't easy to see robots doing what you think only a person could do couple years ago, or accept that an algorithm can take better decisions than a human, or that a production floor can be observed from anywhere in the world. However a blind trust isn't either, it requires strict follow up in the development of the application and knowledgeable personnel to decide correctly what technology makes better fit for the different opportunities. As a leader, we encourage you to use this book as a guideline on what it can be done, how it can be done and start to lead your company into the manufacturing 4.0 journey. As engineer, we encourage you to try, to succeed and also to fail but above all, to never give up.

A big lesson learned along the writing of this book and the implementation of multiple manufacturing 4.0 projects is that even though you'll see the impact in your operation metrics, it is going to be harder to foresee the impact in the environment, so you need to be aware that other ecosystems also change with the implementation of your technology project, and that we live in a interlinked world. Those extra monitors you are planning to use for an electronic dashboard or those scanners to automate data collection will year's later end up in the landfill and you at this moment have a responsibility of purchasing the correct quantity not to save some money for your company but to avoid the unnecessary excess that impacts our world.

References

[1] Exponential manufacturing. Deloitte University Press. 2017

[2] Industry X.0 –Realizing the value in Industrial Sectors. *Eric Schaeffer*, REDLINE Verlag, ©2017.

[3] Augmented Reality. Wikipedia.

[4] Digital Twin. Wikipedia.

[5] Industry 4.0: Managing the Digital Transformation. *Alp Ustundag, Emre Cevikcan*, Springer Series in Advanced Manufacturing, ©2018.

[6] Autonomous Mobile Robots, *Roland Siegwart, Illah Nourabakhsh, Davide Scaramuzza*, MIT Press, Second Edition, 2011.

[7] The Focused Factory, *Wickham Skinner*, Harvard Business Review, May 1974

[8] Lean Thinking, *James P Womack, Daniel T. Jones*, FREE PRESS, ©1996

[9] The Toyota Way, *Jeffrey K. Liker*, McGraw Hill, ©2004.

[10] Applying Manufacturing Execution Systems, Michael McClellan, The St Lucie Press/APICS Series on Resource Management, ©1997

[11] Gartner IT Dictionary. https://www.gartner.com/it-glossary/

[12] The second machine age, *Brynjolfsson and McAfee*, W.W. Norton Company, ©2014

[13] The Principles of Scientific Management, *Frederick W. Taylor*, 1911.

[14] The Machine that Changed the World, *James P. Womack, Daniel T. Jones, and Daniel Roos*, Harper Perennial, ©1990.

[15] The Goal, Eliyahu Goldrath, North River Press, ©1984.

[16] INSIDE OPS – Are your Operations Ready for a Digital Revolution? *Boston Consulting Group*, July 2016.

[17] The Inevitable, *Kevin Kelly*, Penguin Books, ©2016

[18] Building the Internet of Things, *Maciej Kranz*, Wiley, ©2017

[19] Lean Robotics, *Samuel Bouchard*, ©2017

[20] Manufacturing Complexity: A Quantitative Measure, *Lawrence D. Fredendall, T. J. Gabriel*, POMS Conference, April 2003.

[21] *The Rise of Robots* by *Martin Ford*; May 2015, Published by Basic Books.

[22] Organize your future with robotic process automation by PWC

[23] The case for optimism in these strange times by *John Kerry*; June 12, 2017; TIME Magazine.

[24] The World's Workers Have Bigger Problems than a Robot Apocalypse, *Peter Coy*, June 22, Bloomberg Magazine.

[25] Automation, robotics, and the factory of the future by Jonathan Tilley, September 2017, McKinsey & Company.

[26] World Population Ageing 2015, United Nations, 2015.

[27] Japan's Robot Strategy, Headquarters for Japan's Economic Revitalization, 2015.

[28] Global Economy and development at Brookings, *Homi Kharas*, February 2017.

[29] Karel Capek, Wikipedia.

[30] The robot that takes your job should pay taxes, Bill Gates, Interview with Quartz, https://qz.com/911968/bill-gates-the-robot-that-takes-your-job-should-pay-taxes/

[31] The Rise of Robotics, *Alison Sander and Meldon Wolfgang*, August 2014, Boston Consulting Group.

[32] ISO/TS 15066, Robots and Robotic Devices –Collaborative Robots, First Edition 2016-02-15.

[33] Starship Troopers, *Robert A. Heilein*, G. P. Putnam's Sons Publisher, December 1959.

[34] The Technical Trend of the Exoskeleton Robot System for Human Power Assistance, *Heedon Lee, Wansoo Kim, Jungsoo Han, and Changsoo H*, INTERNATIONAL JOURNAL OF PRECISION ENGINEERING AND MANUFACTURING Vol. 13, No. 8, pp. 1491-1497.

[35] Business Insider, *Dylan Love*, August 2014. http://www.businessinsider.com/daewoo-robotic-exoskeletons-2014-8

[36] Dept. of Labor, "Back Injuries - Nation's Number One Workplace Safety Problem", *Fact sheet No OSHA 89-09*, Washington, D.C. GPO, 1999.

[37] Good Materials handling is Good Ergonomics, Modern Materials Handling, Apr. 1999, pp. 56-59.

[38] Bureau of Labor Statistics, Occupational Employment and wages 2005

[39] National Safety Council, Accident Facts 1999, Chicago, IL. Pp. 2,3,33,39.

[40] Robotics in Logistics, A DHL perspective on implications and use cases for the Logistics industry, March 2016.

[41] Trunk Support Exoskeleton, *H. Kazrooni, W. Tung, D. Rempel,*

[42] Springer Handbook of Robotics, Chapter 33 -Exoskeletons for Human Performance Augmentation, *Homayoon Kazerooni*, Springer-Verlag Berlin Heidelberg 2008.

[43] Hype Cycle for Emerging Technologies, 2017, *Gartner*, 21 July 2017.

[44] Design and control of warehouse order picking: A literature review, *De Koster, René et.al.* European Journal of Operational Research. 182(2): 481–50, (2006).

[45] Augmented Reality in Logistics, Changing the way we see logistics – a DHL perspective, 2014.

[46] Industry 4.0 - Enabling Digital Operations, *PwC*, https://i4-0-self-assessment. pwc.nl

[47] Strategic guidance towards Industry 4.0 – a three-stage process model, *Selim Erol, Andreas Schumacher, Wilfried Sihn*, international Conference on Competitive Manufacturing, 2016

[48] Maturity model for assessing Industry 4.0 readiness and maturity of manufacturing enterprises, *SchumAndreas achera, Selim Erol, Wilfried Sihn*, Procedia CIRP 52 (2016) 161 – 166

[49] Skills Needs Analysis for "Industry 4.0" Based on Roadmaps for Smart Systems, *Ernst A. Hartmann, Marc Bovenschulte*, Institute for Innovation and Technology, Berlin, Germany

[50] GE Digital, www.ge.com/digital/insights

[51] Industrie 4.0 Maturity Index -Managing the Digital Transformation of Companies, *Günther Schuh, Reiner Anderl, Jürgen Gausemeier, Michael ten Hompel, Wolfgang Wahlster*, acatech STUDY

[52] Design Principles for Industrie 4.0 Scenarios: A Literature Review, *Hermann, Mario Pentek, Tobias, Otto, Boris*, Technische Universität Dortmund Fakultät Maschinenbau, 2015.

[53] What to do when machines do everything, *Malcom Frank, Paul Roehrig, and Ben Pring*, Wiley, 2016.

[54] AI in the Factory of the Future, *Daniel Kupper, markus Lorenz, Kristian Kulhmann, Oliver Bouffault, Lim Yew Heng, Jon van Wyck, Sebastian Kocher, Jan Schlagater*, BCG, April 2018.

[55] Makers, the new Industrial Revolution by *Chris Anderson*, ©2012, C236rown.

[56] Smart Industry –The IoT Business Magazine, AVNET Silica, 2018.

[57] Making maintenance smarter Predictive maintenance and the digital supply network, *Chris Coleman, Satish Damodaran, Mahesh Chandramouli*, Ed Deuel; A Deloitte series on digital manufacturing enterprises.

[58] Flextronics Will Manage Global Supply Chain with New Real-Time Software, The Wall Street Journal, *Rachel King*, July 7, 2015.

[59] IS the Solow Paradox back? *Mekala Krishnan, Jan Mischke, and Jaana Remes*, McKinsey Quarterly June 2018.

[60] Enterprise resource planning: Implementation procedures and critical success factors. *Umble, E. J., Haft, R. R., and Umble, M. M.*. Eur. J. Opl Res., 2003, 146, 241–257.

[61] Exponential Manufacturing –A collection of perspectives exploring the frontiers of manufacturing and technology, *Deloitte University Press*, ©2017.

[62] Roadmaping for strategy and innovation, Robert Phaal, Clare Farrukh and David Probert, University of Cambridge, ©2010.

[63] The future of spare parts is 3D - A look at the challenges and opportunities of 3D printing, *Reinhard Geissbauer, Jorge Lehr, Jens Wunderlin*, PwC, © 2017

[64] MES Explained: A High Level Vision, *MESA INTERNATIONAL*, -White Paper Number 6, © 1997 Manufacturing Executions Systems Association.

[65] Applying Manufacturing Execution Systems, *Michael McClellan*, the St. Lucie Press/APICS Series on Resources Management, © 1997

[66] A whole new mind –Why right brainers will rule the future, Daniel Pink, 2005

[67] The Impact of technology in Leadership, *Artur Kluz*, World Policy, February 2016.

[68] Good to Great: Why some Companies make the Leap and the Don't', Jim Collins, Harper Business, © 2001

[69] Harnessing the Fourth Industrial Revolution for the Earth, World Economic Forum, November 2017.

About the Authors

Oliver Perez, PhD.

Oliver Perez is Manufacturing Technology Director for Becton, Dickinson and Co. (NYSE:BDX) an American Medical Technology company that manufactures and sells medical devices. He is responsible for achieving maximum efficiencies across BD by the implementation of Manufacturing Technologies. He delivers strategic direction related to the future technologies to be deployed at the different manufacturing sites working in collaboration with the functional leaders.

Prior to joining BD, Dr. Perez held positions of progressive management responsibility in the United States and Mexico within Johnson and Johnson, Accellent and Greatbatch, working in areas of Product Development, Operational Excellence, Engineering, Manufacturing, and Quality Assurance.

Raised in Chihuahua, Mexico, Dr. Perez holds a Bachelor in Science in Electronics Engineering from the Instituto Tecnologico de Chihuahua, Mexico; a Master of Science in Electronics with an Emphasis in Computer Systems from the same Institute; a Doctorate Degree from the University of Henri Poincare of Nancy France with major in Automation and Vision Systems. He is also a certified Black Belt from ASQ, certified PMI, and Lean Enterprise by the University of Michigan. He has authored 2 book chapters and numerous peer-reviewed scientific publications.

Sergio Sauceda, MSc.

Sergio Sauceda is Engineering Manager for BD (Becton, Dickinson and Co.) at Tijuana, Mexico Site for MMS EMI (Electro Mechanical and Instrumentation) Segment. BD manufactures and sells medical devices. He is responsible for achieving operations sustainability, processes improvement & new technologies implementation. He's now in the path for Manufacturing 4.0 implementation at Tijuana site.

With almost 22 years of experience at different industry segments (electronics, aerospace & medical) with experience in test systems development, automation, design for manufacturing applications, process improvement, validation systems and projects management. He has worked for companies as SANYO Manufacturing, EATON Aerospace, FLEX Medical, Greatbatch and CAREFUSION (Now BD) with progressive management responsibilities.

He was born in Mazatlán, Sinaloa, Mexico. Sergio holds a Bachelor Degree in Electronics Engineering from Instituto Tecnologico del Mar at Mazatlán, Mexico; a Master of Science in Control & Automation from CETYS Universidad at Tijuana, Mexico; a Master of Science in Network & Communications from CETYS Universidad at Tijuana Mexico; studies of Master of Administrative Sciences from Instituto Tecnologico de Tijuana; He also holds post grade certs like Six Sigma Black Belt, Lean Manufacturing, Computer Sciences, Mathematical Models, Network server administrator, Data Base Design, Mechanical Design tools and others.

Jesrael Cruz, MSc.

Jesrael Cruz is the Advanced Manufacturing Engineering Supervisor for Becton Dickinson at Tijuana Site. He is responsible for process improvements and new technologies implementations and deploying Manufacturing 4.0 applications across all functional areas of the Tijuana manufacturing site.

With over 16 years of experience in the electronics and medical industry in the development of electrical test systems, automation, robotics and augmented reality applications. He has worked for companies as Sony Electronics, Integer (formerly Greatbatch Medical) and Becton Dickinson.

He was born in Acayucan, Veracruz, Mexico and holds a bachelor's Degree in industrial engineering from Instituto Tecnologico de Tijuana and studies of Master of Engineering Sciences. He is very proficient in object oriented programming, six sigma and lean manufacturing tools, computer sciences, data base design and others.

Printed in the United States
By Bookmasters